The Complete Book of
SALADS

The Complete Book of
SALADS

by

Beryl M. Marton

Illustrations by Grambs Miller

RANDOM HOUSE

NEW YORK

SECOND PRINTING

Copyright © 1969 by Beryl M. Marton

All rights reserved under International and
Pan-American Copyright Conventions.
Published in the United States by Random House, Inc.,
New York, and simultaneously in Canada
by Random House of Canada Limited, Toronto.

Library of Congress Catalog Card Number: 69–16436

Manufactured in the United States of America

Typography and binding design by Mary M. Ahern

To my husband,
MORT,
without whose inspiration this book
would never have been written

FOREWORD

In this unusual book, Beryl Marton has given us a new and personal concept of what constitutes a "salad." She has run the gamut from recipes for plain tossed green salads, familiar to every hostess, to the way-out opinion that even a thick ice-cold soup such as Potage Sénégalese is also a salad.

Out of her rich experience as the head of her own Gourmet Cooking School, Mrs. Marton has written a book of many unusual recipes as well as certain well-known simple ones. They are presented in such concise form that even the novice can follow the directions with assured success, no matter how complicated a recipe may seem upon first reading. The expressions and personal vocabulary reveal the Canadian background of the author, who has been a friend for many years. She displays her understanding of those salads and menus which appeal not only to the hostess who entertains often, but also to the appetites of healthy young teen-agers and husbands.

This is more than a mere salad book. It contains basic hints for the beginner on the fundamentals of becoming a successful homemaker and hostess. Beryl Marton has included recipes that are appealing to the needs of all homemakers, whether they are young brides just beginning to cook and entertain or sophisticated hostesses planning an elaborate buffet. The menus, the ideas, the "know-how" are all here.

Milo Miloradovich
February 3, 1969

Contents

The Complete Book of
SALADS

INTRODUCTION

What is a salad? The definition given by *Larousse Gastronomique* is "Dishes made up of herbs, plants, vegetables, eggs, meat and fish, seasoned with oil, vinegar, salt and pepper, with or without other ingredients." This is a very broad definition and I have broadened it further in this book by adding recipes for certain soups and fruit dishes. I have also added other dishes that can be considered cold entrées and several hot salads with oil-based dressings. In other words, I am including a wide variety of foods that are dressed with an oil and acid sauce. In some, the oil component may be heavy cream, sour cream or mayonnaise (which is, after all, made from oil plus eggs and an acid). The acid ingredient might be lemon juice or wine instead of vinegar. The dressing makes the salad, and the dressing is the basis of my personal definition of "salad."

A salad may be served in a glass bowl or a ceramic bowl, but most people prefer a good deep wooden bowl. Today fine wooden bowls are so finished that they can be washed lightly in soap and warm water. There is a belief that wooden bowls should not be washed. I do not concur. If left unwashed they do, in time, become sticky and rancid. Rubbing the bowl with garlic for savory salads is not a hard-and-fast rule either, in my opinion. If your dressing is well laced with garlic, rubbing the bowl is superfluous. A beautiful wooden bowl with a fine lustrous patina adds great charm to your table setting and, somehow, seems the most appropriate vessel in which to serve your greens.

The presentation of a salad is perhaps as important as the ingredients. Eye appeal adds to one's appreciation of any meal, but enhances the salad supper particularly. Salad is the garnish—the touch of color at the table. It makes the whole meal look more appetizing if it is served thoughtfully. Choose your table appointments carefully, and see to it that the bowl you use complements the other dishes. Always serve tossed salad in an individual bowl or on a separate plate. There is nothing messier than having well-dressed, crisp greens floating around in the Beef Stroganoff.

I would hazard a guess that the ancients ate raw vegetables from the beginning of man's history. I am sure the caveman garnished his raw meat with roots and berries. His mate probably tried to please him with herbs and greens gathered from the forest. We do know the Greeks and Romans served both cooked and uncooked vegetables. The Persians served dressed salads daily. The great Oriental cultures had as many as 365 varieties of vegetables at their disposal. However, the Far Eastern peoples did not use many vegetables raw, to my knowledge. They steamed, dressed and served their foods with great sophistication, but the salad as we know it is an Occidental development.

The earliest book of actual recipes to have survived the passage of time is the work often attributed to Apicius, a famous

Roman gourmet who lived in the first century A.D. The book, entitled *Of Culinary Matters*, mentions salads, dressed lightly, as being "very medicinal." The book also mentions lettuce, parsley, garlic, herbs of every kind and most of the vegetables that grace today's table.

As the great and powerful civilizations collapsed with the coming of the Dark Ages, eating habits, too, deteriorated under the effects of war, ignorance and superstition. As far as we know, very few vegetables were served at the medieval table and virtually no salads were included in the fare. It wasn't until Europe moved into the Renaissance that modern eating habits began to develop.

The first published literary work on salads was *Acetaria, a Discourse of Sallets*, written by John Evelyn and published in 1699. Among the marvelous quotes in this dissertation, my favorite is this: "We are by Sallets to understand a particular Composition of certain Crude and Fresh Herbs, such as usually are, or may safely be eaten with some Acetous Juice, Oyl, Salt, etc. to give them a grateful Gust and Vehicle."

The salad fell out of favor during the eighteenth and nineteenth centuries, all raw vegetables being looked upon with suspicion. However Brillat-Savarin, the great French gastronome (1755–1826), believed that salad "freshens without enfeebling and fortifies without irritating."

In America the pioneer fathers considered the salad as "women's food" and frowned mightily upon it from their strongly masculine position. It wasn't until the twentieth century that the salad regained favor in the public eye. It has steadily gained popularity until today it is one of the most important items on the menu.

Before the coming of refrigeration as we know it today, salads, except for those made with potatoes, cabbage and so on, were served only in the summer months. Now salads of fresh greens are served the year around. Moreover, there are salad-like entrées that are served, hot or cold, as a main course; these salads have been adopted as hearty fare for all seasons.

Most Americans toss and dress the mixed salad at the table and serve it as an accompaniment to the entrée. It becomes, in effect, a vegetable course. Europeans, on the other hand, tend to serve such salads as a separate course, after the main part of the meal and before the dessert. I have also had Caesar Salad, which is much too elaborate to serve as an accessory to a meal, presented as a first course.

My grandfather used to make such a ceremony of tossing a salad that it has become a legend in my family. My grand-mother would meticulously prepare the greens for him and present them, at the table, in a large wooden bowl. Beside the bowl would be one of those old-fashioned casters or cruet sets that we probably all remember seeing as children. Two glass cruets, one with oil, one with vinegar, sat in the rear compart-ment and three small containers of salt, pepper and mustard sat in the front. The whole was encased in a filigree silver basket.

My grandfather, with great care, would measure the oil and sprinkle it over the greens. He believed, like all good salad makers, that the oil should always go first to coat the lettuce. Then he would add the vinegar, salt, pepper and a dash of mustard, in that order. The guests silently watched and ad-mired, and he became known far and wide for his salad-making prowess.

Today, my husband carries on the custom. He has some spe-cialties that he tosses for our guests, and they rather look for-ward to the whole ceremony as part of the Marton tradition.

When and how you serve your salad is entirely up to you. You can open or close the meal with it. It can be appetizer, entrée or dessert—there are no hard-and-fast rules. Use your discretion and serve salad when it complements the rest of the meal, adds beauty and charm to the setting and suits your taste.

CHAPTER 1
Making Salads Work

There are innumerable salad lettuces & other salad greens that can be tossed with great abandon into the salad bowl, & I could perhaps go on for six chapters listing them.

It is
more reasonable,
I think, to list &
discuss only
the ingredients
that are most commonly
found in
American markets.
❨Choose greens
& salad vegetables
that are fresh.
Lettuces & other greens
should be clear in color,
with no bruised spots on the leaves. In buying head lettuces, weigh the head in your hands. The heavier and more
compact it is, the better the buy. Watch for streaks of brown
blight near the root of the head. This may penetrate the whole
vegetable and frequently increases near the core.

Cleaning and storing greens is of the utmost importance.
Three quarters of the battle, as far as a good salad is concerned, is the crispness of the greens. Clean your greens by removing any tough, broken or limp outer leaves. I do not
recommend washing the greens at this point unless you plan
to use them almost immediately, as storing washed greens
tends to hasten the spoiling process. If, however, the vegetables are dirty and you cannot bring yourself to store a bed of
sand in your refrigerator, by all means wash and drain them
thoroughly. Cleaned greens can be stored very well in airtight
plastic containers or the new snap-off plastic bags for a con-
siderable length of time.

Do wash them well before use, as insecticides may have been used in their growing and it is wise to eliminate any traces of the chemicals as well as sand and soil. Several hours before mealtime, wash and shake dry your greens. For this a French salad basket is a must in every household. They are by far the best vegetable drainers on the market, and can be purchased in any good housewares department. Stand the basket on a towel in the refrigerator and allow the greens to crisp in it. If you do not have a French basket, wash the greens, dry on a towel, place several layers of paper toweling at the bottom of the refrigerator crisper and place your salad materials there until ready for use.

Breaking the greens can be done either before or after crisping. Break into bite-size pieces by hand; do not cut. Cutting greens bruises the tender leaves. For a large dinner party it is more convenient to do this job early in the day and allow the salad ingredients to crisp in a large covered container. Each piece should be of a size that is comfortable to eat: nothing is more frustrating than to spear a huge lettuce leaf and to have to try to cut it with your salad fork in the curved bottom of the salad bowl.

After crisping, if any water remains on the leaves, pat them dry with paper toweling (wet greens dilute the dressing) and place them in the salad bowl together with the other ingredients. Toss lightly at the table with the dressing of your choice.

A word about tossing: Another way to bruise tender greens is to toss them too enthusiastically. When I say toss lightly, I mean just that. A gentle touch is imperative in this final, most important step in salad preparation.

THE SALAD KITCHEN

For the bride or beginning cook I might suggest equipment for a "salad kitchen." Listed below is what I have in my kitchen. You may find other items you think are important; by all means don't hesitate to buy them. Every cook acquires favorite methods of preparation and favorite working tools. Buy the basics and keep adding to your equipment, and before you know it, you will be completely equipped.

Chopping Board	Buy a heavy board of unfinished wood. There is an excellent one on the market with a half-cup measuring vessel inserted in one corner which allows you to chop or dice and measure foods in one place.
Chopping Bowl with Metal Chopper	Excellent for chopping eggs, onions, meats, etc. A "must."
Cheesecloth	Keep several packages handy at all times for wrapping foods for poaching, for wrapping herb bouquets and for straining stock and broth.
Colander	This large perforated metal bowl on feet can be used as a crisper if necessary. Excellent for washing and draining vegetables.
Cruets	It is important to have at least two attractive vessels to contain oil and vinegar for dressing salads at the table. An old-fashioned caster may contain vessels for condiments in addition to the oil and vinegar cruets.

Electric Blender	An invaluable addition to any kitchen. It is excellent for making dressings. This should be a new cook's first electric appliance.
Food Mill	Excellent for mashing and grating foods without puréeing them.
French Salad Basket	A folding mesh basket that is easily stored. Very useful for draining and crisping greens.
Garlic Press	A small device used to crush a garlic clove to a purée.
Juicer	Any device that will efficiently squeeze juice from citrus fruits will do.
Mortar and Pestle	This is an optional item, used to pound herbs, spices and condiments to a powder or paste. It is little used in this day and age, but can be most useful in making salad dressings.
Mouli Grater	A marvelous little drumlike revolving grater with a hopper and handle. Eliminates the grating of knuckles when dealing with cheese, chocolate, nuts and so on.
Nutmeg Grater or Mill	Freshly ground nutmeg is superlative. Try it.
Paring Knife	A good, sharp paring knife with a comfortable handle is indispensable.
Pepper Mill	Freshly ground pepper is far superior to the pre-ground kind; every household should have a mill.
Potato Peeler	Excellent for shredding raw vegetables.

Salad Bowl with Servers	Purchase as large a wooden bowl and servers as you can afford. You can serve two from a large bowl, but you can't serve six or eight from a very small bowl.
Individual Salad Bowls	Salad should always be served in separate wooden bowls or on plates.
Chef-Size Salad Bowls	These are optional. They are marvelous for the avid salad-eating family, as a complete-meal salad can be served in each. They are a very elegant and sophisticated touch.
Scissors	Add greatly to the efficiency of any kitchen.
Skewers	Buy large skewers with large heads for easy handling.
Spice Rack	Purchase lined wooden containers that will hold a small quantity of herbs and spices. Lining protects herbs from loss of flavor due to heat, light and air.
String	A ball of strong twine for trussing, tying herb bouquets, etc.
Strainer	At least one good-sized strainer is a necessity in every kitchen. Small ones are handy, too.

GREENS AND LEAFY
VEGETABLES

The greens and leafy vegetables listed below are the ones you will be most likely to use most often in the preparation of salads.

Beet Greens	These can be an interesting addition to a salad, provided they are tender, young and clean. Wash well, cut away any spoiled areas and break into small pieces before or after crisping.
Bibb Lettuce	The finest of all lettuces, Bibb is a miniature head of tender, wavy, dark green leaves, very beautiful in appearance, that adds great elegance to your tossed salad. It is sometimes called limestone lettuce.
Boston Lettuce	Sometimes called butterhead lettuce, Boston and its related varieties have soft-textured, pale green leaves with edges that are a deeper green. It is excellent eating, and also decorative on salad platters.
Chicory	A very curly, slightly prickly, darkish-green head with a white heart. It has a faintly bitter tang that is a welcome change from the bland lettuces.
Dandelion Greens	Early in the spring when young dandelions are just appearing, cut the tiny green plants. Wash well and add the leaves to your salad. When

	the plant is mature, dandelions become too bitter to consume. The young leaves also make a fine cooked vegetable.
Escarole	This is a superior salad green of great beauty, with broad, fairly curly leaves tapering to a prominent whitish base. The texture is tough to the bite, but is excellent in the tossed green salad. The head is loosely knit and fans out into a wide circle.
Fiddleheads	In the early spring when ferns are just on the verge of appearing, go into the damp, darker parts of the forest and part the dead leaves on the floor of the woods. There you will see tiny white, curled fern growths. These are fiddleheads, the most succulent and delicate of edible wild greens. Wash well, removing any fuzz, and steam until tender; then add to the salad bowl. They can also be purchased in bottles in delicacy shops.
Iceberg Lettuce	A firmly packed, round head of pale green leaves, this is easily the most popular of all American market lettuces. It is very crisp in texture and a leaf makes a marvelous cup for holding luncheon salads.
Leaf Lettuce	This is a type of soft-leaved lettuce that includes many varieties ranging in color from pale green to red or bronze. Some form no heads at all;

some make loose heads. Best when very tender and young. Often grown in home gardens.

Nasturtium Leaves   A wonderful addition. They have a peppery, nutty flavor that is delightful. Put tiny whole ones into your salad, or add broken large ones. As a child I used to eat nasturtium and cucumber sandwiches with great relish.

Parsley   Sprigs of crisped curly parsley can be tossed into salads, but I prefer to use it as a garnish. Italian parsley, on the other hand, has larger, flat leaves and a superior flavor. It does not chop as well as the curly kinds, nor does it look as handsome in its natural state. Therefore it is not as desirable as a garnish, but is superior as a flavoring herb.

Romaine   Sometimes called cos lettuce, this is the elite of the lettuce family. Long, beautiful green leaves emerge from a white base. The leaves crisp marvelously and are used as a garnish as well as in many complete-meal salads and tossed salads.

Sorrel   Also known as sour grass, sorrel grows wild in many areas. However, the cultivated French variety is of superior flavor. It has quite an acid taste, and only very young leaves should be added to salads.

Spinach   Raw spinach, well washed and crisped,

makes an excellent green for the bowl. Be sure all the sand is removed from the leaves.

Swiss Chard

The celery-like ribs of chard fan out into spinach-like tops. It is superior in flavor to spinach, in my estimation. One cannot often buy this in the market, but for those ambitious ones, it grows magnificently in almost any garden soil. It is a great vegetable, little known and sadly neglected. Add tops, washed and crisped, to a tossed salad.

Watercress

This delightful clover-like, dark-green miniature leaf has a peppery flavor. Toss the whole sprigs into the bowl. It is an elegant garnish for meat and vegetable dishes. Plan to use soon after purchase, as it won't keep well for more than a day or so.

THE ONION FAMILY & OTHER SAVORY INGREDIENTS

There are any number of different types of onions, but I am listing only the ones I feel are suitable for salads. Go sparingly on the stronger varieties of onion. Avoid serving raw onions in any form unless you are quite familiar with your guests' eating habits. Nothing is sadder than seeing guests methodically picking out ingredients in salads and pushing them aside.

Bermuda and Italian Onions	These huge, mild, beautiful onions are a great addition to salads. Peel and slice very thinly crosswise. Separate into rings. Italian onions are red. Bermudas may be yellow or white.
Chives, Scallions and Shallots	Chop fine and sprinkle over a tossed salad.
Garlic	Never cut garlic directly into a salad. Rub the bowl well with a halved clove before you add greens. If the dressing is well laced with garlic, that should suffice. Do not overdo.
Leeks	Cut into sections, then halve lengthwise and separate layers.
Spanish Onions	These are first cousins of the Bermuda and Italian onions, having the same lovely mild flavor. This onion is a large yellow or white one. It can be used interchangeably with the Italian or Bermuda varieties.

To any combination of greens you can add a number of other vegetables. Many people add sliced radishes and celery to a tossed salad. I prefer not to, as the texture of these vegetables is such that dressings will not adhere to their surface and the cut particles end up scattered in the bottom of the bowl. Belgian endives, Chinese cabbage, cucumbers, fennel, green beans, mild red or green pepper—the possibilities are endless when choosing additions to your green salad. Just remember that nothing should be overdone, so pick additives with care and do not add too many kinds, or too much of any, to your greens.

You will notice that I make no mention of tomatoes in the lists of mixed-salad ingredients. I do not approve of sliced or cut tomatoes in a tossed salad—they tend to weep, diluting the dressing and making the whole salad soggy. The little cherry tomatoes can take their place without the mess. The best way to serve tomatoes, other than the stuffed and otherwise glamorized ways listed in later chapters, is to marinate the sliced or wedge-cut fruit in a good French or vinaigrette dressing, sprinkle with herbs and serve on a lettuce leaf.

Cucumbers may be pared, scored and sliced thin, then added immediately to the salad bowl; or they can be added to the crisper earlier in the day. I think they improve with crisping, but one does not always have the time or forethought to do it. They are good either way.

HERBS AND SPICES

A time-honored definition of an herb is "a plant of which the leaves and stem are used commercially, for medicine, scents, flavorings or food." Spice, on the other hand, is defined as "any aromatic and pungent vegetable substance used for flavoring food." My own working definition is that herbs are the leaves of aromatic and flavorful plants that are usually grown locally like other market-garden produce. Spices are the dried and/or ground berries, leaves, fruits, or other parts of exotic plants that are usually native to warmer climates and exported to consumers in the rest of the world.

Fresh herbs are a welcome addition to any salad, but if you are unable to obtain them or to grow your own, dried herbs can be used quite successfully. A rule of thumb for substituting fresh herbs for dry, or vice versa, is that ¼ teaspoon of powdered or crumbled dried herb equals 1 tablespoon of chopped fresh leaves. When using dried herbs, rub the leaves between your fingertips as you add them to your salad. This helps release the aroma and flavor quickly.

If you are a dweller in the city or the suburbs, you may consider growing a window box full of herbs. One 3- or 4-foot window box, filled with good garden loam, will accommodate six or eight varieties.

Fresh herbs can be prepared for keeping in two ways. You can pick them (just before blooming is the best time), tie them in loose bunches and dry them in a warm, dry place. Rub off the leaves when dry and store in air-tight containers. Or you can chop the fresh herbs and freeze each kind in a small plastic bag. To use, scrape off as large a quantity as is needed from the frozen lump. Frozen herbs are somewhat discolored; however, the flavor remains excellent.

Listed below are only those herbs and spices I feel are useful in salads.

Herbs

Basil	Grows easily in any sunny location. Use ¼ teaspoon dried basil in dressing for salad for 8, or sprinkle 1 tablespoon of the chopped fresh herb over the salad. Often called sweet basil.
Bay Leaf	This is the laurel leaf with which the ancients crowned heroes and victors. Pungent and flavorful, bay leaves are used to flavor marinades, court bouillons, soups, stocks, sauces, etc.
Capers	These are the tiny flower buds of the caper plant, preserved in salt or in brine. They are widely used to flavor and garnish fish as well as in many salads.
Chives	Used constantly in salad preparation, chives can be purchased frozen at the grocer's or may be grown in small pots in the kitchen window. Chive is a delicately flavored plant of the onion family.
Dill	Can often be purchased fresh from the greengrocer. The dried leaves and seeds are available in jars. It is widely used in cookery.
Garlic	This pungent, flavorful bulb is of the lily family and is a close relative of the onion. I need not list its numerous uses.
Marjoram	Grown widely in home herb gardens,

this is a delicate and very popular herb. It can be used dried to flavor any dish you desire, and the fresh leaves, chopped, add greatly to dressings and salads.

Mint Everyone is familiar with the wonderful flavor of mint. It grows well in almost any soil. In fact, care must be taken to contain the planting, as it tends to spread and choke out other vegetation. Especially good in drinks and fruit salads.

Mustard Powdered mustard is made from the dried seeds of certain species of the mustard plant. Other species furnish the tender young leaves that can be either cooked and eaten as a vegetable or added raw to salads.

Oregano This is actually a wild marjoram. With a stronger and more pronounced flavor, it is more widely used than sweet marjoram.

Parsley Can be purchased in any produce market. There are two principal types, the tight, beautiful, curly kind which makes a fine garnish, and the flat-leaved Italian parsley, of superior flavor but less appealing to the eye.

Rosemary Fresh rosemary is very difficult to find. It will grow as an annual in your garden or as a tender perennial that must be brought indoors in cold winter climates. Fresh rosemary is lovely in fruit drinks and in salads. Use with discretion, as a very little gives enough flavor.

Sage
This is a very hardy perennial which grows satisfactorily in any garden. Extremely versatile, this herb is used in many kinds of cookery. A very little fresh sage is marvelous added to the salad bowl, but caution must be used, as sage is strong and tends to have a slightly bitter and medicinal flavor.

Tarragon
One of the most popular herbs, with endless uses. A pinch of fresh or dried tarragon will do wonders for many dressings.

Thyme
The best culinary thyme is a tiny, hardy shrub with needle-like leaves, often called "common thyme." This is the form dried for sale. Sometimes used in cooking, too, is creeping thyme, which makes a wonderful ground cover. Thyme sprigs can be used whole to give flavor to soups and braised dishes, and may be steeped in dressings.

Spices

Cayenne	A very hot pepper. Use sparingly.
Cloves	Ground clove is used mainly to flavor sweet foods, but has its uses with savory foods too. The whole clove is inserted into ham, fruits, etc., so that its flavor permeates the food as it cooks.
Curry Powder	This is usually a very hot combination of ground spices that originated in India. Use sparingly in dressings, soups and sauces.
Ginger	This is sold powdered, fresh, candied or dried. Its pungent, peppery flavor does wonders for fruit salads, but use with discretion—it is powerful.
Nutmeg	May be purchased ground, but I prefer grating my own in a nutmeg grinder. The warm spicy flavor is very good in fruit mixtures.
Paprika	Purchased ground in shaker jars, this spice adds a delicate flavor when sprinkled as a garnish on potato or fish salads.
Pepper	Buy jars of whole peppercorns and grind fresh as needed in a pepper mill.
White Pepper	Available whole or ground. This is the kernel of the peppercorn. Used when black pepper would be unsightly, as in white sauces.

CHAPTER 2

Sundry Tossed Salads

The
tossed salad
is probably
the most popular
of all salads; when good,
it can be the making
of a meal.
The choice of ingredients
& the proper cleaning &
crisping of the greens
are discussed in
the preceding chapter.

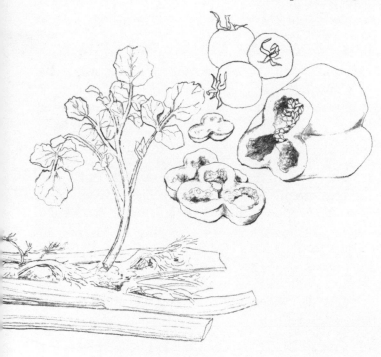

Recipes
for basic dressings
& many variations
are in Chapter 3.
(Following are recipes
for a number
of basic tossed salads.
You may want to try
your own variations—
by all means do so.
Don't be afraid
to try new ideas.
If you feel more
comfortable practicing on your family before you entertain,
do so, but don't tell them you are experimenting. Present
your salad as a *fait accompli*.

As a general rule you will find that two heads of a compact
variety of lettuce, with various flavoring additives, will serve
eight people. Do not dress your greens too copiously; too much
dressing will make the salad soggy. If there is an accumulation
of dressing in the bottom of the bowl you have overdone it.
Each leaf should be well coated with the dressing, but not
dripping. As an approximate guide, I would suggest that you
use about ½ to ⅔ cup of dressing on green salad for eight.

Marinating is often called for in the recipes that follow. A
word here as to technique: Whenever possible it is advisable
to pour the marinade over cooked vegetables while they are
still warm and allow them to cool in the marinade. The marinade will permeate the vegetables to a far greater extent when
they are warm and the cells are expanded.

If you plan to double any of the recipes, remember that not

all ingredients should be doubled—it is necessary to use discretion. A good example of such an ingredient is the anchovy. If a recipe to serve 8 calls for 2 full cans of anchovies and you wish to serve 16, you would double the basic ingredients. However, 4 cans of anchovies would probably give too strong a flavor, so I would suggest the use of only 3 cans. The same caution is called for in adding dressing when doubling a recipe. Make double the amount, but have the salad tosser add the dressing gradually, using judgment as to the amount needed.

Cherry-Tomato Salad

A wonderful salad to serve with steak or roast beef.

1 head romaine lettuce
½ head chicory
½ head iceberg lettuce
2 trimmed Belgian endives
1 cucumber
1 green pepper, seeded and cut in rings
Handful of cherry tomatoes
½ cup French dressing with Roquefort, page 45

Wash the romaine, chicory and iceberg lettuce and place in the refrigerator to crisp. Slice the endives lengthwise into julienne strips. Cut ends from cucumber and slice off long strips of skin lengthwise, leaving alternating bands unpeeled. Score the peeled areas with the tines of a fork and slice cucumber into ⅛-inch slices. Add, along with the endives, to the crisping greens. Cut ends off green pepper, remove seeds and slice in very thin rings. Just before serving, pat greens dry on paper towels if necessary, being careful not to bruise or crush the leaves. Break into bite-size pieces. Place in a large wooden bowl and add the washed tomatoes. Toss lightly with dressing. Serve immediately. *8 servings.*

Raw Mushroom Salad

Serve this salad with a casserole supper. The raw mushrooms become quite a topic of conversation.

1 head escarole
½ head Boston lettuce
½ head iceberg lettuce
1 peeled, scored and sliced cucumber
½ pound raw mushrooms
1 Bermuda *or* Spanish onion
½ cup Basic French Dressing, page 44
3 tablespoons chopped parsley

Wash, crisp and break greens. Add cucumber to crisper. Wipe mushrooms with damp cloth. Peel if they are discolored—if not, leave skins on. Trim stems to within ¼ inch of cap. (Reserve stems and peels for the soup pot.) Cut mushrooms in thin slices and set aside. Just before serving, place greens and cucumber in salad bowl, top with mushrooms and slice the onion thinly over all. Toss with dressing at the table. Sprinkle with parsley and serve at once. *8 servings.*

Avocado Salad

1 pound fresh spinach
1 avocado
1 tablespoon lemon juice
1 onion
2 tablespoons dairy sour cream
1 clove garlic, crushed

Remove stems from spinach, wash thoroughly and crisp in refrigerator. Peel and dice avocado (sprinkle with lemon juice to prevent discoloring). Slice onion as thin as possible and separate rings. Place sour cream, garlic, salt, lemon peel, paprika, pepper, vinegar and oil in a screw-top jar and shake vigorously to blend. Place spinach, avocado and onion rings in a

¼ teaspoon salt
½ teaspoon grated
   lemon peel
¼ teaspoon paprika
¼ teaspoon pepper
2 tablespoons tarra-
   gon vinegar
½ cup olive oil
6 slices bacon,
   cooked until crisp

salad bowl, pour in dressing and toss lightly. Crumble bacon over top and serve. *6 to 8 servings.*

Raw Asparagus Salad

Serve with steak or barbecued spareribs.

12 stalks raw aspara-
   gus
½ small head red
   cabbage
1 head romaine,
   washed and
   crisped
1 head chicory,
   washed and
   crisped
1 cucumber, peeled
   and scored
⅔ cup Lemon
   French Dressing,
   page 46

Wash asparagus spears and snap off the green upper part. Reserve tips to use as a vegetable—we are concerned with the lower, tougher stalks. Cut off the very white ends and discard. Cut remaining stalks into 2-inch pieces. Peel the thin green outer skin off and discard. Slice each 2-inch piece into very fine julienne strips. Set aside.

Cut red cabbage into wedges and remove the inner core. Slice each wedge very fine as for cole slaw, removing or shredding all thick pieces.

Break romaine and chicory into bite-size pieces. Slice cucumber into thin circles. Place all ingredients in a salad bowl and toss with the dressing. *8 servings.*

Watercress Salad

Serve this salad with baked or poached fish.

1 head Boston lettuce
½ head chicory
½ head romaine lettuce
8 leaves spinach
1 bunch watercress
1 avocado
½ cup French dressing with capers, page 44

Wash, crisp and break lettuces, chicory and spinach. Wash and crisp watercress. Cut avocado in half, peel and remove pit. Slice in thin strips, or dice. Break off long stems of cress and add the whole sprigs, with the other greens, to the bowl. Toss with the well-shaken dressing and serve at once. *8 servings.*

Artichoke-Heart Salad

Excellent with baked or roasted chicken.

1 head Bibb lettuce
1 head escarole
1 cucumber
2 cups cooked and halved artichoke hearts
1 cup Basic French Dressing, page 44
½ head fennel
1 cup thinly sliced Bermuda *or* Italian onion

Wash, crisp and break greens. Slice and crisp cucumber. Marinate the canned, fresh or frozen cooked artichoke hearts in ½ cup French dressing for at least 2 hours. Cut fennel stalks into 2-inch pieces and slice lengthwise into ¼-inch julienne strips. Drain the artichoke hearts and place with all other ingredients in a salad bowl. Toss with the remaining ½ cup dressing and serve immediately. *8 servings.*

Garlic-Crouton and Leek Salad

Try this salad next time you have a barbecue.

4 slices white bread
4 tablespoons butter
2 cloves garlic, crushed
1 head romaine lettuce
1 head escarole
3 leeks
4 stalks Chinese cabbage
1 cup black olives, pitted
½ cup French dressing with onion, page 45

Garlic Croutons: Remove crusts from bread. Cut bread into ¼-inch cubes. Melt butter in a skillet. When sizzling add crushed garlic and cook, stirring, 1 minute without browning. Add the bread cubes and sauté, tossing frequently to prevent burning, until golden brown. Drain on paper toweling and cool.

Wash, crisp and break greens. Slice white part of leeks into 1-inch pieces, then cut pieces lengthwise into halves. Separate leeks into flat sections, discarding any bruised ones. Wash well and drain. Set aside. Cut Chinese cabbage into 2-inch pieces and cut lengthwise into ¼-inch julienne strips. Place greens, leeks, Chinese cabbage, black olives and croutons in a deep salad bowl. Toss lightly with dressing and serve immediately. *8 servings.*

Herbed Green Salad with Asparagus Bits

Serve this salad with leg of spring lamb.

1 head romaine lettuce
1 head Bibb lettuce
½ head iceberg lettuce
1 cup fresh or frozen asparagus, sliced
½ cup Basic French Dressing, page 44
½ cup French dressing with tomato, page 45
2 tablespoons chopped fresh dill
2 tablespoons chopped fresh tarragon

Wash, crisp and break greens. Cook fresh or frozen asparagus until barely tender. Drain, then marinate in Basic French Dressing for at least 2 hours. Drain well. Place with greens in bowl. At table toss with tomato-flavored French dressing and sprinkle with herbs, or sprinkle each individual helping with a few pinches of the finely chopped dill and tarragon. 8 *servings.*

Oriental Tossed Salad

Great with barbecued chicken.

1 head romaine
1 head Boston lettuce
3 stalks Chinese cabbage
4 water chestnuts

Clean, crisp and break lettuces. Trim leaves from Chinese cabbage and cut stalks into 3-inch pieces. Slice these into julienne strips about ⅛ inch thick. Slice water chestnuts thin. Add soy sauce to dressing and shake well.

1¼ cups cooked,
drained bean
sprouts, *or*
canned bean
sprouts, rinsed
and drained
1 tablespoon soy
sauce
½ cup Basic
French Dressing,
page 44

Toss all ingredients together lightly
with dressing and serve immediately.
8 servings.

Mediterranean Tossed Salad

A natural with Italian or Spanish dishes.

1 head romaine let-
tuce
1 head escarole
4 stalks fennel
1 can (2 ounces)
anchovy fillets
1 tablespoon may-
onnaise
½ cup French dress-
ing with capers,
page 44
¼ cup chopped wal-
nuts
½ cup grated Parme-
san cheese

Clean, crisp and break lettuce and escarole. Trim tops off, cut fennel into
3-inch pieces, then into julienne strips
¼ inch thick. Drain and chop the
anchovies. Add mayonnaise to caper
dressing and mix well. Place greens,
anchovies, walnuts and cheese in a
wooden salad bowl. Toss with dressing and serve immediately. *8 servings.*

Sorrel Salad

Good with pot roast or braised beef.

1 head iceberg lettuce
1 head romaine
2 stalks fennel
3 or 4 leaves of young sorrel
½ cup Basic French Dressing, page 44
1 tablespoon chopped chives
1 tablespoon chopped parsley
1 tablespoon chopped fresh tarragon

Clean, crisp and break lettuces. Trim tops off and cut fennel into 3-inch pieces, then into julienne strips ¼ inch thick. Cut sorrel into fairly small pieces. Place lettuces, fennel and sorrel in a bowl and toss with dressing. Sprinkle with chives, parsley and tarragon and serve at once. *8 servings.*

Dandelion-Green Salad

This should be served only in early spring, when dandelions are at their best.

1 cup very young, tender dandelion greens
1 head iceberg lettuce
1 head romaine lettuce
2 tomatoes

Dandelion greens can be very bitter if they are too mature, so pick only the youngest, most tender ones. Carefully wash and crisp them. Wash, crisp and break lettuces. Peel tomatoes by dipping them in boiling water for 2 or 3 seconds, then slipping off skins. Cut in half and remove all seeds

1 Spanish onion
1 cucumber, peeled and scored
⅔ cup Green Goddess Dressing, page 52

and center pulp. Cut tomato flesh into strips and drain well on paper toweling. Slice onion and cucumber. Place all ingredients in a salad bowl and toss with dressing. *8 servings.*

Tangy Tossed Salad

This is good with duck, pork or lamb.

1 head romaine lettuce
1 head iceberg lettuce
1 can (8 ounces) mandarin oranges, drained
1 cup fresh or canned grapefruit sections, drained
1 cup sliced fresh oranges, drained
4 tablespoons olive oil
2 tablespoons vinegar
¼ teaspoon salt
½ cup currant jelly
3 scallions, green tops and all, chopped

Wash, crisp and break greens. Place in a wooden bowl with drained fruits. Place oil, vinegar, salt and currant jelly in a blender and whirl until thoroughly blended. (If you do not have a blender, heat mixture until jelly melts, then cool before using.) Sprinkle salad with scallions and toss with dressing. *8 servings.*

Nasturtium-Leaf Salad

This salad can be served only in the summer, as nasturtiums are annuals.

1 head iceberg lettuce
½ head chicory
1 head Boston lettuce
16 small nasturtium leaves, 1 inch in diameter
1 small Bermuda onion
1 cup raw fresh peas
½ cup French dressing with tomato, page 45

Wash, crisp and break greens. Wash nasturtium leaves well and pat dry on paper toweling. Slice Bermuda onion thin. Place greens, nasturtium leaves, onion slices and peas in a salad bowl and toss lightly with the dressing. *8 servings.*

Bacon and Egg Tossed Salad

Try this salad the next time you serve veal or fish.

½ head chicory
1 head escarole
1 head romaine
8 rashers bacon
¼ cup bacon fat
¼ cup olive oil
1 to 2 tablespoons vinegar
Salt, to taste

Clean, crisp and break greens. Dice bacon and fry until crisp. Reserve fat and drain bacon well on paper toweling. Measure ¼ cup bacon fat, add olive oil, vinegar, salt and pepper, parsley, chives and rosemary. Place in a screw-top jar and shake vigorously. Slice eggs and cucumber. Place in a salad bowl with the greens. Toss with

Freshly ground
pepper, to taste
1 tablespoon
chopped parsley
1 tablespoon
chopped chives
1 tablespoon
chopped fresh
rosemary, *or* ¼
teaspoon dried
rosemary
2 hard-cooked eggs
1 cucumber

dressing and sprinkle with bacon just
before serving. *8 servings.*

Waldorf Salad

This is rather an elegant salad, a trifle rich. I would suggest serving it with a standing rib roast or a crown roast of pork.

1 cup diced celery
1 cup diced red
apples, unpeeled
1 cup seedless green
grapes, halved
½ cup chopped wal-
nuts
½ cup mayonnaise
¼ cup dry vermouth
3 tablespoons
chopped fresh
mint

Place celery, apples, grapes and walnuts in a small wooden salad bowl.
Mix mayonnaise with vermouth and
pour over the fruit. Toss lightly.
Sprinkle with chopped fresh mint.
8 servings.

CHAPTER 3

The "Gust and Vehicle" of the Salad

Dressings and Their Preparation

As I
have stated previously,
the dressing,
called by John Evelyn
the "gust & vehicle,"
is the most important
single ingredient
of a salad.
A good dressing
can make a salad &
a poor one can ruin it,
no matter how fine
your greens are.

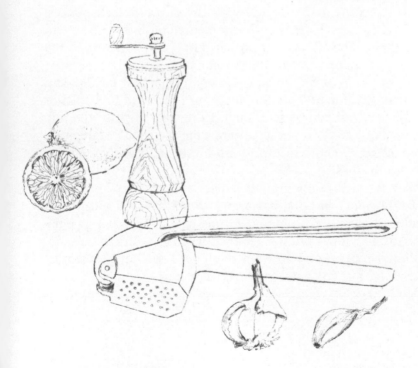

There are
a few firm rules
concerning the dressing
of salads; I list them
below.
❨As mentioned
in the previous chapter,
it is important
not to use
too much dressing.
❨About ½ to ⅔ cup
will be enough
to dress greens
for 8 servings. Always remember to add the oil first, if you
are making the dressing at the table directly in the salad
bowl. Toss the greens lightly with the oil until each piece is
well coated; otherwise, the vinegar poured onto the greens will
wilt them. The oil serves a further purpose in adhering to the
leaf: it causes other seasonings to cling, too.

In dressings of the French (vinaigrette) type I have used a
basic proportion of 1 part of vinegar or other acid to 4 parts of
oil; however, if you prefer a tangier dressing, increase the proportion of acid. You can substitute wine or lemon or lime juice
for vinegar. Do not use a wine as a substitute if you are serving
it with the meal.

Always use freshly ground pepper from your pepper mill.
The difference in taste, flavor and aroma between pre-ground
and fresh pepper is stunning. All the volatile oils that give flavor to the peppercorn are retained when it is freshly ground.
White pepper is ground from the inner kernel of the peppercorn after the dark outer husk has been removed.

All the dressings for which recipes follow will improve with time. They should be made several hours in advance and allowed to ripen. You can refrigerate most of them for several days; but you should bring them to room temperature before serving. Dressings do not freeze well.

Do not dress a green salad until you are ready to serve it. If greens are allowed to stand in the dressing for too long, they tend to become very soggy and unappetizing.

I prefer using a good imported olive oil in all dressings; however, other salad oils may be used instead. Vegetable oils are quite adequate for mayonnaise. Vinegars should be of a good wine or cider variety. At the end of this chapter there are suggestions on how to prepare and flavor your own vinegars. Flavored vinegars keep well and can add interesting taste changes to your meals. They also make thoughtful and pleasant gifts for your gourmet friends. If you grow your own herbs, experiment to your heart's content. If not, try dried herbs.

Basic French Dressing

1 cup good im-
   ported olive oil
¼ to ⅓ cup wine
   vinegar, according
   to taste
1 teaspoon salt
¼ teaspoon freshly
   ground pepper
½ teaspoon dry mus-
   tard

Place all ingredients in a screw-top jar and shake vigorously. Allow to mellow at least 1 hour and shake well before using. It will keep in the refrigerator for at least one week. *Makes 1¼ cups.*

Variations of French Dressing

To recipe for Basic French Dressing, add:

Anchovy

Mash a 2-ounce can of anchovy fillets and add, along with oil from anchovies. *Makes 1½ cups.*

Avocado

Mash avocado to make ¼ cup and add. Add ½ teaspoon Worcestershire sauce. *Makes 1½ cups.*

Caper

Crumble 2 hard-cooked egg yolks and add. Add 1 tablespoon chopped capers, 1 crushed clove of garlic, ¼ teaspoon paprika and a dash of Tabasco. *Makes 1½ cups.*

Cranberry

Add 2 tablespoons chopped raw cranberries. *Makes 1⅓ cups.*

Curry

Chop very fine enough chutney to make 2 tablespoons and add. Add 1 chopped hard-cooked egg and ½ teaspoon curry powder. *Makes 1½ cups.*

Herb	Chop 1 tablespoon each parsley, chives and fresh dill. Add to basic dressing and allow to mellow for several hours. *Makes 1¼ cups.*
Mint	Add 2 tablespoons chopped fresh mint and ½ teaspoon Worcestershire sauce. *Makes 1⅓ cups.*
Nut	Add ¼ cup chopped almonds, walnuts or pistachios. *Makes 1½ cups.*
Onion	Stud a medium-sized onion with 5 or 6 cloves and bake in a moderate oven (350° F.) until tender when pierced with a fork. Cool and discard cloves. Chop onion very fine and add to basic dressing. *Makes 1½ cups.*
Roquefort	Mash ⅓ cup crumbled Roquefort or Danish Blue cheese and add to basic dressing. *Makes 1⅔ cups.*
Tomato	Purée 2 tomatoes by forcing through a sieve or whirling in the blender. Place in a saucepan and rapidly boil down to one half the quantity. Strain and add to dressing with 1 crushed garlic clove. *Makes 1¾ cups.*

Lemon French Dressing

⅔ cup olive oil
⅓ cup fresh lemon juice
¼ teaspoon sugar
⅓ teaspoon freshly ground pepper
1 garlic clove, crushed
¼ teaspoon dry mustard
1 teaspoon salt

Place all ingredients in a screw-top jar and shake vigorously until blended. *Makes 1 cup.*

Basic Mayonnaise

Homemade mayonnaise should be made in a blender, otherwise it becomes an endless job of beating, beating, beating. The secret of good mayonnaise is to add the oil very slowly while beating the eggs vigorously, thus allowing the egg and oil to emulsify. I prefer using all vegetable oil or half olive oil and half vegetable oil. I do not care for the overpowering taste of olive oil alone, but this is a matter of taste.

2 eggs
¼ cup wine vinegar
1 teaspoon salt
Dash of freshly ground pepper
¼ teaspoon dry mustard

Place the eggs, half the vinegar, and all of the salt, pepper and mustard in the blender jar. Whirl this mixture together at top speed to blend, then start adding half the oil drop by drop. When the emulsion starts to thicken, add oil in a steady stream. The may-

1 cup vegetable oil
  or olive oil

onnaise will become quite thick. At this point add the remaining vinegar. Then start adding the remaining oil slowly until all has been incorporated. Refrigerate for future use. *Makes approximately 2 cups.*

Variations of Mayonnaise

To one cup of mayonnaise, add:

Caviar

Add ½ cup sour cream, 1 jar (4 ounces) red caviar and 2 tablespoons dry white wine. *Makes approximately 2 cups.*

Cottage Cheese

Add ½ cup cottage cheese, forced through a sieve or whirled in a blender, 1 tablespoon chopped dill and a dash of Tabasco. *Makes 1½ cups.*

Green

Add ½ cup puréed spinach or ½ cup puréed green peas. This makes a marvelous masking sauce for cold fish. *Makes 1½ cups.*

Herb

Add 1 teaspoon each chopped parsley, watercress and chives, ¼ teaspoon each dried tarragon and basil. Allow to blend flavors for several hours before use. *Makes 1 cup.*

English Mayonnaise

2 mashed hard-
cooked egg yolks
1 raw egg
¼ cup wine vinegar
1 teaspoon salt
Freshly ground
pepper
¼ teaspoon dry
mustard
⅓ cup olive oil
⅔ cup sweet cream

Place mashed hard-cooked egg yolks and raw egg in blender. Add vinegar, salt, pepper and mustard. Blend for a moment on high speed, then gradually add oil, then cream, using same method as for basic mayonnaise (page 46). *Makes approximately 2 cups.*

Russian Dressing

1 cup mayonnaise
3 tablespoons bot-
tled chili sauce
1 teaspoon chopped
pimiento
1 teaspoon chopped
chives
¼ cup chopped
olives
¼ teaspoon Wor-
cestershire sauce
1 hard-cooked egg,
chopped
1 to 2 tablespoons
cream

Place all ingredients in a screw-top jar and shake. Thin with as much cream as desired. *Makes 1½ cups.*

Mystère Dressing

A very *rich dressing. Serve only with salads accompanying broiled or roasted meats.*

¾ cup heavy cream
1 cup mayonnaise
4 tablespoons prepared horseradish
2 cloves garlic, crushed
4 tablespoons chopped chives
2 tablespoons chopped parsley
2 drops of Tabasco

Whip cream. Mix together mayonnaise, horseradish, garlic, chives and parsley. Fold into whipped cream. Add Tabasco. *Makes 2½ cups.*

Bacon Salad Dressing

2 tablespoons bacon fat
1 tablespoon flour
½ cup boiling water
2 eggs
1 tablespoon lemon juice
1 teaspoon sugar
1 teaspoon dry mustard
½ cup vinegar
Salt, to taste
Freshly ground pepper, to taste

Place bacon fat in a skillet and heat until bubbling. Add flour and cook 2 to 3 minutes, stirring constantly and not allowing to brown. Off the heat add boiling water, beating with a wire whip. Return to heat and bring to a boil. Beat eggs with remaining ingredients. Off the heat, add small amount of hot liquid to eggs, beating constantly, then add egg mixture to hot mixture very slowly, stirring the while. Cook, stirring, 2 to 3 minutes. Cool, stirring constantly. Correct seasoning. *Makes 1½ cups.*

Parmesan Dressing

2 hard-cooked egg
  yolks
4 tablespoons olive
  oil
1 tablespoon grated
  Parmesan cheese
1 teaspoon prepared
  mustard
1 tablespoon tar-
  ragon vinegar
  Dash of Worces-
  tershire sauce
  Salt
  Freshly ground
  pepper

Mash egg yolks with oil. Blend in cheese, mustard, vinegar and Worcestershire sauce. Add salt and pepper to taste. *Makes ½ cup.*

Boiled Salad Dressing I

To use with cole slaw and potato salads.

3 eggs
1 cup light cream *or*
  milk
¼ cup vinegar
1 teaspoon dry
  mustard
2 teaspoons salt
¼ teaspoon freshly
  ground pepper

Beat eggs until lemon-colored. Add other ingredients, mixing well. Cook in double boiler over medium heat until thick, stirring constantly. Cool, stirring to prevent skin forming. If too thick, add a few drops of oil or milk. *Makes 2 cups.*

Boiled Salad Dressing II

8 egg yolks
2 cups cream *or* milk
1 cup vinegar
2 teaspoons sugar
2 teaspoons salt
½ teaspoon pepper
1 teaspoon dry mustard
2 tablespoons oil

Beat egg yolks well and add cream or milk. Add vinegar and sugar and cook approximately 5 minutes in a double boiler over medium heat; stir constantly until thick. Remove from heat and add salt and pepper. Mix mustard with oil and stir into dressing. Cool, stirring occasionally to prevent skin from forming. *Makes 3 cups.*

German Salad Dressing

1 clove garlic, chopped
2 tablespoons chopped onion
½ cup vinegar
1 cup dairy sour cream
2 teaspoons superfine sugar
¼ teaspoon white pepper
2 teaspoons salt
1 teaspoon dry mustard
4 tablespoons bacon fat

Place garlic, onion and vinegar in a saucepan. Bring to a simmer and cook, covered, until vegetables are tender. Mix together sour cream, sugar, pepper, salt, mustard and bacon fat and beat into cooked mixture.

This dressing is good with potato salad or a salad of equal parts of chopped celery and apple. *Makes 2 cups.*

Green Goddess or Sour-Cream Dressing

Serve this dressing on a green salad accompanying a plain roast or a broiled steak.

½ cup mayonnaise
¼ cup dairy sour cream
2 teaspoons lemon juice
½ tube (2-ounce size) anchovy paste
3 tablespoons tarragon vinegar
¼ cup chopped parsley
·1 clove garlic, crushed
3 tablespoons crumbled blue cheese (*optional*)

Place all ingredients in a screw-top jar and shake vigorously. Allow dressing to mature for several hours before serving. Will keep in the refrigerator for several days. *Makes approximately 1½ cups.*

Anchovy Dressing

1 can (2 ounces) anchovies
4 tablespoons oil
1 teaspoon prepared mustard
1 teaspoon capers
1 tablespoon vinegar
1 clove garlic, crushed

Mash anchovies with 1 tablespoon of the oil and the mustard. Add remaining ingredients and shake or beat well. Thin further with oil if necessary. *Makes ½ cup.*

Roquefort Creole Dressing

1 egg
2 cloves garlic, crushed
⅛ teaspoon salt
½ cup olive oil
1 teaspoon lemon juice
1 tablespoon wine vinegar
¼ pound Roquefort cheese, crumbled
Freshly ground pepper

Place egg, garlic and salt in blender. While blending at moderate speed, add half of the oil very slowly. When thick add lemon juice, then remaining oil and vinegar. Fold in cheese and add pepper to taste. *Makes approximately 1 cup.*

Dressing for Potato Salad

1 tablespoon butter
1 tablespoon flour
1½ cups boiling milk
1 teaspoon salt
Pepper, to taste
2 egg yolks *or* 1 whole egg
2 to 3 tablespoons tarragon vinegar
1 tablespoon chopped chives

Melt butter in skillet and add flour. Cook 2 to 3 minutes without browning. Off the heat, add milk all at once, beating with a wire whip. Add salt and pepper to taste. Return to heat and cook, stirring, 5 minutes. Beat egg with vinegar. Gradually add a small amount of the hot liquid to eggs, then gradually, stirring constantly, add eggs to milk mixture. Cool, stirring occasionally, then add chives. Toss with cooled cooked potatoes. *Makes 2 cups.*

Sardine Dressing

1 egg
1 can (3¾ ounces) sardines in oil
4 tablespoons olive oil
2 tablespoons vinegar
1 teaspoon dry mustard
¾ teaspoon salt, or more if needed
¼ teaspoon pepper
2 tablespoons chopped parsley

Beat egg very well. Mash sardines in their oil and add to egg. Beat in olive oil and vinegar, then remaining ingredients. Excellent on a green salad accompanying a fish dinner. *Makes ½ cup.*

Tomato Dressing

2 tablespoons butter
1 small green pepper, seeded and chopped
1 onion, sliced
Dash of cayenne
2 cups chopped fresh tomatoes
1 teaspoon cornstarch
1 teaspoon salt
1 clove garlic, chopped

Melt butter in a skillet and sauté green pepper and onion. Add cayenne. When brownish, add tomatoes and cook until very soft. Whirl in a blender, or force through a sieve. Strain through cheesecloth and put purée in a saucepan. Bring to a boil. Blend cornstarch into a small amount of water and add to purée, stirring constantly. Add salt and garlic. Simmer ½ hour. Cool. *Makes approximately 1 cup.*

Harlequin Dressing

¼ cup chopped
cooked beets
¾ cup olive oil
3 tablespoons white
wine vinegar
1 hard-cooked egg,
chopped
1 teaspoon paprika
1 teaspoon salt
3 tablespoons
lemon juice
1 tablespoon
chopped parsley
1 teaspoon sugar
½ teaspoon dry
mustard
Dash of Tabasco

Drain chopped beets well on several thicknesses of paper toweling. Place all ingredients in a screw-top jar and shake well. Allow to blend for ½ hour or more. *Makes 1¼ cups.*

East Indian Dressing

2 hard-cooked egg
yolks
8 tablespoons olive
oil
2 tablespoons vine-
gar
1 teaspoon curry
powder
Salt, to taste
1 tablespoon finely
chopped candied
ginger

Mash egg yolks. Add oil, vinegar and curry powder. Add salt to taste, then add ginger. *Makes ½ cup.*

Greek Dressing

½ cup blanched almonds
¾ cup olive oil
Juice of 1 lemon
Freshly ground pepper
1 boiled potato, mashed
1 tablespoon vinegar
1 teaspoon salt
3 cloves garlic, pressed
½ cup dry white wine, or as needed

Place nuts and half of the oil in a blender. Whir until nuts are in very fine particles. Add remaining oil and lemon juice. Add pepper, potato, vinegar, salt and garlic and blend until smooth. Add wine until of desired consistency. *Makes 1½ cups.*

Chef's Salad Dressing

1 clove garlic, crushed
½ cup olive oil
1 teaspoon salt
2 tablespoons vinegar
½ cup mayonnaise

Place all dressing ingredients in a screw-top jar and shake vigorously. Pour into a cruet and pass with the salad. *Makes 1 cup.*

Horseradish Cocktail Dressing

1 cup bottled chili
sauce
1 tablespoon Wor-
cestershire sauce
2 to 3 tablespoons
prepared horse-
radish, depending
on taste
1 tablespoon lemon
juice

Stir together well and serve. *Makes 1½ cups.*

DRESSINGS FOR FRUIT SALADS

Mayonnaise-based Dressings

To 1 cup of mayonnaise add any one of the following:

1. 3 mashed bananas and 1 cup heavy cream, whipped. *Makes 2½ cups.*
2. 4 tablespoons chopped chutney. *Makes 1⅛ cups.*
3. 2 tablespoons chopped raw cranberries, 2 tablespoons dairy sour cream and 2 tablespoons superfine sugar. *Makes 1½ cups.*
4. 1 cup crushed strawberries and 1 tablespoon sugar. *Makes 2 cups.*
5. ½ cup honey, 1 tablespoon lemon juice, ½ teaspoon celery seed. *Makes 1½ cups.*

Simple Dressings

1. Juice of 2 lemons and 2 tablespoons honey. *Makes ½ cup.*
2. White of 1 egg, beaten until frothy and mixed with 1 tablespoon sugar and ½ cup crushed almonds. *Makes ⅔ cup.*
3. Steep 1 sliced lemon in ½ cup claret for at least 4 to 5 hours. Strain and use claret as dressing. *Makes ½ cup.*
4. Place in blender 2 tablespoons oil, 1 tablespoon vinegar, dash of salt and ¼ cup currant jelly. Whirl until blended. *Makes ½ cup.*

Almond Dressing I

½ cup ground
blanched almonds
1 to 2 tablespoons
sherry
½ cup heavy cream,
whipped

Mix almonds and sherry into a paste. Fold in whipped cream. Serve over a salad of peaches, cantaloupe and pears. *Makes 1½ cups.*

Almond Dressing II

2 tablespoons al-
mond paste
1 cup water
Pinch of salt
3 tablespoons sugar
2 tablespoons melted
butter
2 tablespoons lemon
juice

Place almond paste, water, salt and sugar in a saucepan and cook until thick. Remove from heat and add butter and lemon juice. Cool. *Makes approximately 1 cup.*

Sherry Dressing

⅔ cup olive oil
3 tablespoons vine-
gar
4 tablespoons sherry
2 tablespoons
honey
½ teaspoon salt

Combine all ingredients and mix well. *Makes 1⅓ cups.*

Fruit Salad Dressing

Juice of ½ lemon
½ cup pineapple juice
2 teaspoons sugar
2 egg yolks
½ cup heavy cream, whipped
Dash of nutmeg

Heat to boiling lemon juice, pineapple juice and sugar. Remove from heat. Beat egg yolks well and add a small amount of the hot syrup slowly. Return this heated mixture to the hot syrup, beating constantly with a wire whip. Return to low heat and cook until thickened. Cool. Fold in whipped cream and a dash of nutmeg. *Makes 1½ cups.*

Ruby Red Salad Dressing

This dressing is especially good over a macédoine of fresh fruit.

1 package (3 ounces) cream cheese
2 tablespoons cream
1 tablespoon lemon juice
Dash of salt
3 tablespoons currant jelly
¾ cup heavy cream, whipped

Mash cream cheese and add cream and lemon juice. Add salt and whip in currant jelly. Fold in whipped cream. *Makes 1½ to 2 cups.*

French Fruit-Salad Dressing

¼ cup grapefruit
juice
2 tablespoons
lemon juice
½ cup olive oil
⅓ teaspoon paprika
⅛ teaspoon salt
2 tablespoons
chopped candied
pineapple
1 tablespoon
chopped candied
cherries

Place all ingredients in a screw-top jar and shake vigorously. *Makes approximately 1 cup.*

Coconut Cream Dressing

A favorite with coconut lovers.

1 tablespoon lime
juice
½ cup sherry
1 cup unsweetened
coconut
2 tablespoons sugar
3 tablespoons salad
oil

Place lime juice and sherry in a blender and add coconut. Whirl until puréed. Fold in sugar and oil. *Makes approximately 1 cup.*

Citrus Fruit Dressing I

These Citrus Fruit Dressings can be used to dress greens as well as fruits.

1 tablespoon port *or* sherry
½ teaspoon salt
1 tablespoon sugar
3 tablespoons olive oil
Dash of cayenne

Place all together in a screw-top jar and shake vigorously. Allow to blend for several hours and shake well before serving over orange and grapefruit wedges. *Makes approximately ¼ cup.*

Citrus Fruit Dressing II

1 egg, beaten
½ cup sugar
1 tablespoon grated orange peel
2 teaspoons grated lemon peel
Juice of 1 lemon
Juice of 1 orange
1 cup mayonnaise

Place egg, sugar, grated fruit peels and juices in a double boiler. Cook, stirring constantly, over medium heat until thick. Cool and fold in mayonnaise. *Makes approximately 1½ cups.*

Tangy Fruit Dressing

½ cup Boiled Salad
Dressing I,
page 50
Juice of ½ lemon
2 teaspoons sugar
½ cup dairy sour
cream
Juice of ½ lime

Mix all together well and serve over fresh fruits. *Makes approximately 1¼ cups.*

Honey-Lime Mayonnaise

2 eggs
⅓ cup honey
½ teaspoon grated
lime peel
¼ cup sugar
1 teaspoon dry
mustard
1 teaspoon paprika
¼ teaspoon salt
1 teaspoon celery
seed
⅓ cup lime juice
1 cup salad oil

Using method for preparing mayonnaise (page 46), place eggs, honey, lime peel, sugar and seasonings in blender jar. Add half of the lime juice and begin blending. Gradually add half of the oil. Add remaining lime juice and as much of the remaining oil as needed for desired consistency. Good with any fruits. *Makes approximately 2 to 2½ cups.*

LOW-CALORIE DRESSINGS

For weight watchers I am including several excellent dietetic recipes. Most low-calorie dressings are either too insipid or too vinegary, but I have found those given below to be both appetizing and appropriate. The calorie count per tablespoon is given, as a tablespoonful of dressing is adequate for the average serving of salad.

Cottage-Cheese Mustard Dressing

2 tablespoons powdered nondairy creamer
Warm water
1 tablespoon sugar or 4 saccharin tablets
½ cup cottage cheese
3 tablespoons vinegar
1 egg yolk
1 teaspoon salt
Dash of pepper
1 tablespoon prepared mustard
2 cloves garlic, crushed

Place powdered nondairy creamer in a cup and add enough warm water to make ¼ cup liquid. Add saccharin tablets or sugar and dissolve. Place all ingredients in a blender and whirl until well mixed.

If you do not have a blender, press cheese through a sieve and beat in remaining ingredients. *Makes 1 cup.*

15 calories per tablespoon if made with sugar
12 calories per tablespoon if made with saccharin

Garlic Dressing

2 tablespoons cornstarch
¾ cup water
2 tablespoons salad oil
¼ cup vinegar
¾ teaspoon salt
1½ teaspoons sugar
1 teaspoon prepared horseradish
1¼ teaspoon prepared mustard
½ teaspoon Worcestershire sauce
½ teaspoon paprika
¼ cup catsup
1 clove garlic, crushed

Mix cornstarch in a small amount of the water until smooth. Bring remaining water to boil and slowly add cornstarch, stirring constantly. When thick and clear remove from heat and cool. Beat in all the remaining ingredients except garlic. When well blended, add the garlic which has been crushed through a garlic press. *Makes approximately 1½ cups.*

20 calories per tablespoon

Variations of Garlic Dressing

Egg   Add mashed yolk of one hard-cooked egg.

Caper   Add 1 tablespoon chopped capers.

Onion   Add 1 small onion, grated.

Mayonnaise Substitute

2 hard-cooked egg
  yolks
2 egg yolks
1 cup plain yogurt
1 teaspoon lemon
  juice
1 teaspoon chopped
  chives
½ teaspoon salt
  Dash of freshly
  ground pepper
4 saccharin tablets,
  crushed

Mash hard-cooked egg yolks. Beat in raw egg yolks. Stir in remaining ingredients and refrigerate. *Makes 1½ cups.*

18 calories per tablespoon

Variations of Mayonnaise Substitute

Dill
Add 1 teaspoon chopped fresh dill and 1 tablespoon chopped dill pickle.

Russian
Add 2 tablespoons tomato catsup, 1 clove crushed garlic and a dash of paprika.

Herb
Add 1 teaspoon each chopped parsley and chives and ½ teaspoon fresh basil, chopped.

Caper
Add 1 tablespoon chopped capers and 1 clove crushed garlic.

Curried Yogurt Dressing

1 cup plain yogurt
¼ cup chopped celery leaves
¼ cup chopped parsley
¼ cup mayonnaise
3 minced scallions
1 tablespoon prepared horseradish
1 teaspoon salt
Freshly ground pepper
2 teaspoons sugar
1 teaspoon curry powder
Juice of ½ lemon

Beat all ingredients together, or place in a blender and whirl. *Makes 1¼ cups.*

15 calories per tablespoon

Cooked Salad Dressing

½ cup vinegar
3 egg yolks
½ teaspoon prepared mustard
⅛ teaspoon salt
Dash of cayenne
⅛ teaspoon paprika
1 teaspoon sugar
1 clove garlic, crushed

Heat vinegar to boiling. Beat egg yolks and very slowly add vinegar, beating constantly. Cook in double boiler over medium heat until thick, stirring. Remove from heat and cool. Add remaining ingredients and refrigerate. *Makes ¾ cup.*

17 calories per tablespoon

Mock French Dressing

2 tablespoons water
2 tablespoons vine-
gar
2 tablespoons lemon
juice
½ medium onion,
minced
2 tablespoons sugar
½ teaspoon salt
¼ teaspoon dry
mustard
Freshly ground
pepper

Place all ingredients in a screw-top jar and shake vigorously. *Makes ⅔ cup.*
4 calories per tablespoon

Buttermilk Herb Dressing

1 cup buttermilk
1 teaspoon chopped
chives
1 teaspoon chopped
watercress
1 clove garlic,
crushed
½ teaspoon chopped
tarragon
¼ teaspoon dry
mustard
½ teaspoon salt
Freshly ground
pepper
½ teaspoon sugar

Place all ingredients in a screw-top jar and shake vigorously. Chill and serve. *Makes approximately 1 cup.*
10 calories per tablespoon

Spicy Tomato Dressing

1 cup tomato juice	Place all ingredients in a screw-top jar
2 tablespoons red wine vinegar	and shake. *Makes 1¼ cups.*
1 clove garlic, crushed	*8 calories per tablespoon*
½ teaspoon chopped parsley	
½ teaspoon chopped chives	
¼ teaspoon dry mustard	
½ teaspoon salt Freshly ground pepper	
1 tablespoon sugar	

Variations of Spicy Tomato Dressing

Cucumber	Add ½ cup finely chopped cucumber.
Onion	Add 1 small onion, grated.
Egg	Add 1 hard-cooked egg, finely chopped. *Increase calorie content to 10 calories per tablespoon*

MAKING YOUR OWN
VINEGARS

The making of your own vinegar and flavoring vinegar with herbs and spices are actually easy processes; however, patience is of the utmost importance. You cannot rush the procedure. All you need is a large, old-fashioned crock, cider or malt vinegar, a supply of wine, and various herbs, spices and patience. It takes about a month for herbed vinegar to take on sufficient flavor. At the end of this period the vinegar is strained, bottled (in sterilized bottles) and sealed or corked.

Choose the prettiest bottles you can find and place a sprig of the herb you are using in the bottle. Homemade gifts are the greatest compliment you can pay a friend. Try the following recipes and watch your friends' reactions.

Basil and Garlic Wine Vinegar

Pick enough fresh basil to fill a 2-quart crock loosely. Pour enough cider vinegar over basil to fill crock and allow to steep, covered, for 2 weeks. At the end of this perod strain vinegar through several layers of cheesecloth and discard basil. Refill crock with basil and once more pour the vinegar over the leaves. Slice 2 cloves of garlic into the crock. Allow to stand, covered, for 10 more days. Strain vinegar. Add 2 cups of dry red wine.

Sterilize 2 one-quart clear glass bottles. Fill with vinegar. Force a sprig of dried basil into bottle and drop in 1 cut clove of garlic. Seal with a small amount of melted paraffin, as you would preserves, or cork tightly. Label bottles and set aside. Will keep indefinitely. *Makes 2 quarts.*

Spiced Vinegar

4 quarts cider vinegar
6 cloves garlic
6 slices onion
1 tablespoon powdered ginger
1 tablespoon prepared horseradish
1 tablespoon mustard seed
1 tablespoon peppercorns
1 tablespoon whole allspice

Place all ingredients in a heavy enamel pot and simmer, covered, 10 hours. Strain and bottle as for Basil and Garlic Wine Vinegar, above. *Makes 4 quarts.*

Pure Wine Vinegar

2 cups wine of your choice, red or white
Small amount of "mother" (fermentation-causing substance) obtained from an old bottle of vinegar

Place wine and "mother" in a jar and keep in a cool, dark place for 5 to 6 months. Taste vinegar at the end of 5 months and judge whether you need to ferment it further. If not, remove the "mother" and place in a small jar with some of the vinegar; reserve for future use. (Never discard "mother," as it may be hard to obtain when you want it.) Strain the vinegar through several thicknesses of cheesecloth and bottle in sterilized containers. This makes the finest of wine vinegars. *Makes 1 pint.*

Thyme-Scented Claret Vinegar

Following the procedure above, use 1½ pints distilled (white) or malt vinegar, ½ pint cider vinegar, 1 cup claret wine, 1 cup fresh thyme and 2 cloves garlic. Steep 2 weeks, then strain. Put fresh thyme in crock and return vinegar. Slice in 2 fresh cloves of garlic. Let stand 10 more days. Strain and bottle as directed above, placing a sprig of dried thyme, if available, in each bottle. *Makes 1½ quarts.*

❧ BASIC SAUCES ❧

The two sauces that follow are used in the preparation of several salads listed in subsequent chapters.

Velouté Sauce

3 tablespoons
minced onion
3 tablespoons butter
2 tablespoons flour
2 cups boiling veal
stock
1 teaspoon salt
Freshly ground
pepper, to taste

Sauté onion in melted butter for 5 minutes without browning. Add flour and cook, stirring constantly, 2 to 3 minutes. Off the heat add boiling veal stock all at once, beating vigorously with a wire whip. Add salt and pepper and cook over medium heat 5 more minutes. *Makes 2 cups.*

Béchamel Sauce

This is the basic white sauce used in innumerable dishes. For a thicker sauce, increase proportions of butter and flour.

2 tablespoons butter
2 tablespoons flour
2 cups milk
1 teaspoon salt
Freshly ground
pepper

Melt butter, add flour and cook 2 to 3 minutes without browning, stirring constantly. Bring milk to a boil in a saucepan and add all at once to the roux, beating vigorously with a wire whip. Add salt and pepper. Cook, stirring, for 5 minutes over medium heat. *Makes 2 cups.*

CHAPTER 4

Sophisticated Salad Snacks
Antipasto, Smörgåsbord and Hors d'Oeuvre

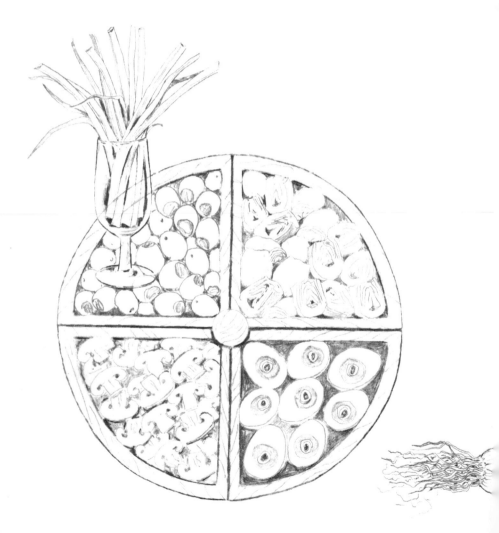

M any hors d'oeuvre & foods of the same type that are traditional parts of the Italian antipasto & the Swedish smörgåsbord are obviously members of the great family of salads.

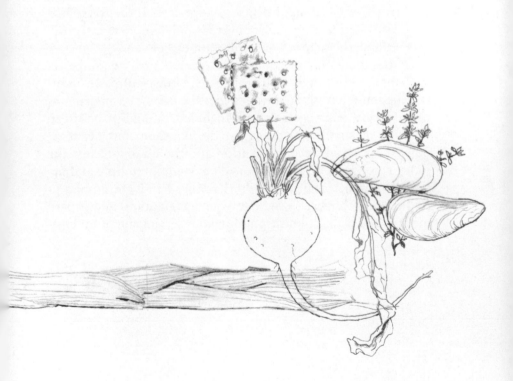

Because of this
I am including
a selection
of these cold dishes
in this salad cookbook.
Serve them as
a first course, either
at table or on a buffet;
or present them on
an appetizer tray
set out with drinks.
([Always remember
that the appearance
of your tray is of utmost importance at the cocktail hour.
An attractive selection of delicious appetizers is the foretelling
of great things to come; or if cocktails only are served, the tidbits become the focus of your entertaining.

Of the foods that are traditional elements of the antipasto,
the smörgåsbord and the hors d'oeuvre tray, antipasto items
are the most refreshing and perhaps the easiest to prepare, as
many greens and vegetables are included. A smörgåsbord can
be large or small, depending on the occasion, but often re-
quires a bit of advance preparation and the finding of just the
right ingredients. Elaborate hors d'oeuvre require time and patience to prepare; but many, on the other hand, are simpler to
fix than they appear to be. Use your imagination, and experiment in the choice of dishes and in your serving appointments.

ANTIPASTO

Line a large platter or tray with crisp greens. Arrange on them a handsome selection of the vegetables, meats, fish and garnishes listed below. Place cups of iceberg or Boston lettuce on the platter to hold a mound of Chick-Pea Salad, page 80.

Meats, Fish and Cheese

Anchovies	Either flat fillets or the rolled, caper-stuffed kind.
Bologna	Serve either sliced or cut into cubes.
Cheese	Thin slices of provolone or Parmesan, or wedges of gorgonzola.
Capocollo	Smoked pork. Slice paper-thin and roll up. Can be found in Italian food stores.
Italian Sausage	Purchase at an Italian delicatessen. Try the hot variety known as *salsiccia con peperoni,* or just "peperoni," or the dry type called *salsiccia secca.* Both are very highly spiced—serve in thin slices.
Prosciutto	Slice wafer-thin and roll up.
Salami	Slice thin, or cut into cubes.
Sardines	Buy sardines in oil or in tomato sauce. I prefer the boned variety.

Vegetables

Artichokes	Cook a 9-ounce package of frozen artichoke hearts à la grecque (page 117), or purchase a jar of marinated artichokes.
Beets	Cook, skin and slice ⅛ inch thick. Marinate at least 24 hours in ½ cup vinegar, ½ cup water and 2 tablespoons sugar boiled together for 5 minutes.
Carrots	Scrape carrots and trim ends. Using a vegetable peeler, cut thin lengthwise slices. Place in ice water for several hours to curl.
Celery	Clean and quarter hearts. Cut stalks into julienne strips, or stuff them (page 124).
Cucumbers	Slice and marinate in 1 part water to 2 parts vinegar and a dash of sugar.
Fennel or Finocchio	Licorice-flavored, celery-like vegetable of Italian origin. A great antipasto favorite. Serve as you would celery hearts.
Green Peppers	Clean and cut into rings, or prepare à la grecque, page 115.
Hard-cooked Eggs (Deviled Eggs)	Quarter or halve eggs and remove yolks. Mash yolks with enough mayonnaise to moisten, then add approximately ¼ teaspoon prepared mustard per egg. Mound yolks into whites.

Lettuce	Iceberg, Boston and Bibb for lining the platter.
Olives	Serve any variety.
Pimientos	Buy in jars. Drain and cut into strips or rings.
Radishes	Clean and trim off tops. Make rosettes by slicing from the trimmed end thin slivers of the red almost to the bottom, leaving attached there. Chill in a shallow pan of ice water for several hours to curl the flowers.
Scallions	Clean and cut off part of green tops, leaving scallions about 6 inches long.
Tomatoes	Use small cherry tomatoes if in season. Otherwise peel and slice large tomatoes, or cut into wedges. If very juicy, drain well on paper toweling.

Chick-Pea Salad

1 cup dried chick
  peas (garbanzos)
1 quart water
1 teaspoon salt
3 tablespoons
  chopped chives
¼ cup mayonnaise
¼ cup Basic French
  Dressing, page 44
1 clove garlic,
  crushed
Juice of ½ lemon
Salt, to taste
Freshly ground
  pepper, to taste

Soak chick peas overnight in water. In morning bring to boil slowly and simmer until tender, approximately 45 to 50 minutes, adding salt when half done. Mix remaining ingredients together and toss with drained, cooled chick peas. Chill well. *8 servings.*

Stuffed Leeks

1 bunch leeks (4 or
  5 leeks)
1 can (7 ounces)
  crab meat
1 tablespoon
  minced parsley
½ cup finely diced
  celery
½ cup mayonnaise
  Juice of ½ lemon

Clean leeks and cut off all green tops. Remove roots but leave base plate intact. Drop into boiling salted water and cook until barely tender, 15 to 20 minutes. Drain well and cool. Cut off bases and push out centers of leeks, leaving tubes. Pick over and mash crab meat and add remaining ingredients. Stuff leek casings carefully and chill. *6 to 8 servings.*

THE SMÖRGÅSBORD

The smörgåsbord is the Swedish equivalent of the antipasto in that both are basically appetizer courses, but it is quite different in content. Few fresh vegetables are included, perhaps because of the colder climate and shorter growing season. The smörgåsbord is a great array of pickled, seasoned and dressed fish and other seafoods, meats, eggs, cheeses, and vegetables. Many of these are prepared as salads. Guests serve themselves from the multitude of hot and cold dishes. The full-scale smörgåsbord can be considered a buffet meal rather than an appetizer course. Because of this it is marvelously versatile for parties. The clever hostess can prepare all the dishes ahead of time and bank a huge buffet table with beautifully dressed platters (and, if she likes, hot dishes on warming stands) that will serve a large number of guests. Aspics are quite suitable for the smörgåsbord—see Chapter 7 for ideas.

The following recipes are mainly for meat and fish dishes, including salads, that are to be served in company with breads, cheeses, vegetables, relishes and condiments. Some accompaniments might be marinated herring, pickled mushrooms, cold ham, cold meat loaf thinly sliced, caviar butter with black bread, pickled fruit such as crabapples, pears or plums, fruit gelatin cut into squares, a bowl of fresh fruit salad, seasoned cottage cheese and goat's cheese. If hot dishes are to be served, Swedish meat balls and baked beans are traditional and very good.

Herring and Beet Delight

2 salt herrings
1 cup cider vinegar
½ cup sugar
1 onion, thinly sliced
Freshly ground pepper, to taste
Sauce (*below*)
2 jars (1 pound) tiny whole beets, drained
Sprig of parsley

Soak herrings overnight. Remove skin and bones. Cut into 1-inch pieces and place in a ceramic, glass or plastic bowl (do not use metal). Bring vinegar and sugar to a boil and simmer, stirring, until sugar dissolves. Cool and add onion and pepper. Pour over fish and marinate 4 to 5 hours. Drain herring and onion and arrange on a platter. Mask with the chilled sauce. Garnish with the tiny beets and a sprig of parsley. *8 average servings, or 12 to 14 smörgåsbord servings.*

Sauce:

2 teaspoons cornstarch
1 cup water
½ teaspoon salt
Freshly ground pepper, to taste
2 teaspoons prepared horseradish
1 to 2 teaspoons sugar
Juice of 1 lemon
2 egg yolks
½ cup dairy sour cream
Chopped parsley, to taste

Mix cornstarch with a small amount of the water. Bring remaining water to a boil and stir in the dissolved starch. Cook until thickened. Add salt, pepper, horseradish, sugar and lemon juice (sauce will be thin). Beat egg yolks. Add small amount of sauce to eggs, beating constantly with a whisk; then, off the heat, beat warmed eggs into rest of sauce. Return to very low heat and stir constantly until thickened. Do not allow to boil or sauce will curdle. Cool, then fold in the sour cream and parsley. Taste to correct the seasoning. Sauce should be sharply sweet and sour.

Poached Perch in Caviar Sauce

3 pounds ocean
   perch fillets
1 carrot, cut in 1-
   inch pieces
½ onion, sliced
2 or 3 sprigs parsley
½ bay leaf
2 or 3 celery tops
5 whole pepper-
   corns
1 teaspoon salt
2 to 3 cups water
   Sauce (*below*)
3 dill pickles, sliced
3 tablespoons
   chopped parsley

Place all ingredients but the fish, sauce and garnish in a large kettle. Lay fish carefully on top of the vegetables. Bring to a boil, lower heat and poach, covered, approximately 15 minutes, or until fish will flake easily. Remove fillets carefully and set aside. Strain fish broth and reserve. Add enough water to make 2 cups.

Arrange poached fish on a platter and mask with sauce. Garnish with sliced dill pickles and chopped parsley. *8 average servings, or 12 to 14 smörgåsbord servings.*

Sauce:

3 tablespoons butter
3 tablespoon flour
2 cups boiling fish
   stock (*above*)
½ cup heavy cream
2 tablespoons black
   caviar
1 teaspoon chopped
   dill pickle
   Salt, to taste
   Freshly ground
   pepper, to taste

Melt butter, stir in flour and cook 2 or 3 minutes, stirring. Off the heat, add boiling stock while beating vigorously. Cook over low heat until thickened. Cool. Whip cream until it will hold soft peaks, then fold into cooled sauce. Fold in caviar and dill pickle. Season to taste.

Masked Salmon with Eggs

3 to 4 pounds salmon from center cut of fish
Cheesecloth and string
1 carrot, cut in ½-inch pieces
1 onion, quartered
2 or 3 celery tops
2 or 3 parsley sprigs
4 or 5 peppercorns
1 teaspoon salt
1 bay leaf
1 quart water

Wrap salmon in 2 layers of cheesecloth and tie ends. Place vegetables and seasonings in a large kettle equipped with a rack. Pour in water, then lay salmon on rack. Bring to a boil and simmer, covered, 30 minutes. Cool in the broth. Remove fish and discard cheesecloth and string. Remove skin and bones carefully from fish. Cool fish and set aside. Strain fish broth and reserve for future use (it freezes well).

Sauce:

1 cup mayonnaise
½ cup sieved, cooked green peas
4 hard-cooked eggs, sliced
Chopped parsley

To mask fish: Blend mayonnaise well with mashed green peas and smooth carefully over the salmon. Arrange slices of hard-cooked egg around the salmon. Garnish with chopped parsley. *8 average servings, or 12 to 14 smörgåsbord servings.*

Mussel Salad

3 dozen mussels
1 onion
1 tablespoon butter

Scrub mussels well, removing all beards. Soak in cold water. Drain; discard any open mussels that will

1 bay leaf
¼ teaspoon dried
thyme
½ cup dry white
wine
½ cup mayonnaise
Lettuce, washed
and crisped

not close when tapped sharply. Slice onion and place in a kettle with butter, bay leaf, thyme and wine. Add the mussels, cover and cook over high heat, shaking the pot, for approximately 5 minutes, at which point mussels should all be open. Remove from pot, reserving liquid, and cool. Shell and set meat aside.

Strain the mussel broth through doubled cheesecloth, then reduce by boiling until a few tablespoons remain. Cool, then stir into the mayonnaise. Toss the mussels with the mayonnaise and arrange on lettuce leaves. *6 servings as an appetizer.*

Anchovy Salad

1 onion, chopped
3 tablespoons butter
Pinch of sugar
2 cans (2 ounces
each) anchovy
fillets, chopped
3 hard-cooked eggs,
chopped
Freshly ground
pepper, to taste
1 can (2 ounces)
rolled, stuffed an-
chovies

Sauté onion in butter with a pinch of sugar. Remove from heat and scrape into a bowl. Add chopped anchovies and chopped eggs. Season with pepper. Shape into a mound on a large round dish and garnish with rolled, stuffed fillets of anchovy. Circle with disks of rye bread and serve. *6 servings as an appetizer.*

Herring Salad

2 salt herrings
1½ cups cooked veal,
pork *or* lamb,
chopped
1½ cups cooked
beets, well
drained and
diced
3 raw apples, diced
2 dill pickles, diced
5 tablespoons wine
vinegar
2 tablespoons
sugar
Freshly ground
pepper, to taste
¼ cup dairy sour
cream
2 hard-cooked
eggs, sliced
Chopped parsley

Soak herrings overnight. Remove all skin and bones. Taste for saltiness; if too salty soak in milk for 2 to 3 hours. Drain and chop into small bits. Combine with meat, beets, apples and pickles. Add vinegar, sugar and pepper. Toss lightly, then bind with sour cream. Oil a fish-shaped mold and press herring salad firmly into it. Chill. Turn out on an oval platter and garnish with slices of hard-cooked egg and chopped parsley. *8 average servings, or 12 to 14 smörgåsbord servings.*

Pickled Cucumbers

3 large cucumbers
1½ cups cider vinegar
1 cup sugar
½ teaspoon salt
Freshly ground
pepper, to taste

Peel and slice cucumbers. Bring vinegar, sugar and seasonings to a boil, stirring until sugar is dissolved. Pour over cucumbers and marinate at least 2 hours. *8 servings.*

Stuffed Cold Beets

8 large beets, cooked and skinned
½ cup cooked, chopped ham *or* tongue
2 hard-cooked eggs
2 scallions
Mayonnaise to bind
1 teaspoon prepared horseradish
Glaze (*below*)
1 hard-cooked egg, sliced
Dairy sour cream

Scoop out centers of beets with a spoon, leaving a shell about ¼ inch thick. Chop beet centers, meat, eggs, and scallions fine. Add mayonnaise and horseradish and stuff beet shells carefully.

Glaze:

1 envelope (1 tablespoon) unflavored gelatin
¼ cup water *or* beet juice
¼ cup vinegar
¼ cup sugar
½ teaspoon salt

Soak gelatin in water or beet juice; then add vinegar, sugar and salt. Heat, stirring, until gelatin and sugar dissolve. Cool, then refrigerate until it begins to thicken. Glaze each beet with a spoonful of the gelatin mixture. Allow to set. (If remaining glaze gets too thick to pour, heat gently until it melts.) Place a slice of egg on top of each beet and glaze again. Top with a scoop of sour cream. *8 servings.*

Chopped Liver

This is a typical American-Jewish appetizer that lends itself admirably to the smörgåsbord.

½ pound chicken livers
1 onion, chopped
5 to 6 tablespoons chicken fat
2 hard-cooked eggs
1 teaspoon salt
Freshly ground pepper, to taste
Lettuce, washed and crisped
2 tomatoes

Sauté chicken livers and onion in 3 tablespoons of the chicken fat until cooked. Chicken livers should be slightly pink in the middle and onions limp. This takes approximately 10 minutes. Place in a chopping bowl with the eggs. (Some people use an electric blender at this point, but the chopped liver loses its character when too well blended.) Chop eggs, onion and liver together until of a very fine consistency. Add salt and pepper to taste and bind with remaining chicken fat. Arrange on lettuce leaves and garnish with slices or wedges of peeled tomato. *8 servings as an appetizer.*

Vegetable Mold

2 envelopes (2 tablespoons) unflavored gelatin
½ cup cold water
1 cup tomato juice
2 cups chicken bouillon

Soak gelatin in cold water. Bring tomato juice and bouillon to the boil and stir in gelatin and sherry. Cool, then place in refrigerator. When just beginning to thicken, fold in grated cabbage, chopped celery, grated carrot and sliced radishes. Turn into a

2 tablespoons dry
sherry
1 cup grated cab-
bage
½ cup chopped
celery
1 cup grated carrot
Several radishes,
sliced
Lettuce, washed
and crisped
Black olives
Scallions

rinsed and chilled 1½-quart mold. Chill until set. Unmold on a bed of lettuce and garnish with black olives and scallions. *8 servings.*

Swedish Mushrooms

2 pounds white but-
ton mushrooms
⅔ cup olive oil
⅓ cup lemon juice
½ teaspoon salt
Freshly ground
pepper, to taste
2 cloves garlic
¼ teaspoon dry
mustard

Trim and wipe mushrooms. (Use only the small white ones that do not require peeling.) Place remaining ingredients and mushrooms in a crock or enamel pot. Marinate, tossing occasionally, for at least 12 hours. *8 to 10 servings.*

☙ HORS D'OEUVRE ❧

In European restaurants hors d'oeuvre are served in marvelous drumlike affairs with moving layers of baskets filled to the top with all kinds of dressed goodies. The waiter wheels this array over to the table and one commences to gorge oneself with the most marvelous tidbits. I, personally, enjoy the hors d'oeuvre tray more than any other course served. The recipes that follow are only a sampling of what can adorn your tray. Each hors d'oeuvre is, of course, presented in a separate dish.

I would suggest that you provide a bread basket or tray containing several kinds of breads and crackers to accompany hors d'oeuvre. A good bread tray might include a loaf of thinly sliced black bread or a seeded rye, some melba toast, saltine crackers, thin slices of French bread, toasted and buttered, and a handful of bread slices.

The dishes for which recipes follow would stock an hors d'oeuvre tray to serve 18 to 20 people adequately. Each recipe, alone, yields the indicated servings.

Marinated Mushrooms

2 pounds small white mushrooms
2½ cups vinegar
¾ cup olive oil
3 cloves garlic, crushed
2 tablespoons chopped parsley

Remove stems from mushrooms and reserve for another use. Wipe mushrooms clean and parboil in salted water for 3 or 4 minutes. Drain well.

Place all remaining ingredients in a saucepan, bring to a boil and cook 10 minutes. Pour over mushroom caps, cool, cover and marinate in the refrigerator for 4 or 5 days. These can

1 bay leaf
Pinch of dried
thyme
½ teaspoon fennel
seed
Freshly ground
pepper, to taste

be bottled for the preserve shelf or served on the hors d'oeuvre tray. *8 servings.*

Beet and Apple Hors d'Oeuvre

3 or 4 cooked
beets, depending
on size
1 large tart apple
½ cup Basic French
Dressing, page 44
1 tablespoon
chopped chives

Chop beets and apple very fine. Toss with French dressing. Arrange in a small dish and sprinkle with chopped chives. *6 servings.*

Smoked Beef Hors d'Oeuvre

2 large kosher dill
pickles
1 jar (5 ounces)
chipped smoked
beef
1 package cream
cheese

Cut dill pickles into strips 1½ inch long and ½ inch wide. Spread slices of smoked beef with softened cheese and wrap around strips of pickle. Chill. *8 servings.*

Artichoke Hearts

3 tablespoons olive oil
1 tablespoon vinegar
1 teaspoon salt
Freshly ground pepper, to taste
1 package (9 ounces) frozen artichoke hearts
1 teaspoon celery seed
1 small jar (8 ounces) pickled beets, well drained

Put oil, vinegar, salt and pepper in a saucepan. Add artichoke hearts, cover tightly and cook just until tender. Remove artichoke hearts and slice. Return to marinade and cool, then chill. Sprinkle celery seed over hearts. Chop drained beets. Arrange chilled, drained artichokes in a dish and surround with beets. *8 servings*.

Anchovies and Egg

3 hard-cooked eggs
2 cans (2 ounces each) anchovy fillets
2 teaspoons capers
1 tablespoon chopped parsley

Separate hard-cooked egg whites from yolks. Chop whites fine and place in small serving dish. Drain oil from anchovies over the egg whites and toss lightly. Dice anchovy fillets and sprinkle over egg whites. Crumble or sieve egg yolks over fillets. Sprinkle capers over all and garnish dish with parsley. *6 servings*.

Caviar and Sour Cream

1 jar (3¾ ounces)
black caviar
½ pint dairy sour
cream
1 tablespoon grated
onion
Thin slices of
black bread

Stir caviar, sour cream and onion together. Turn into a dish and serve with small squares of black bread. *6 servings.*

Smoked Salmon with Egg

¼ pound smoked
salmon
¼ pound mush-
rooms, chopped
1 tablespoon butter
1 green pepper,
chopped
½ cup dairy sour
cream
1 tablespoon
chopped chives
Dash of Tabasco
2 hard-cooked eggs,
finely chopped

Cut salmon into ¼-inch pieces. Sauté mushrooms in butter for 5 minutes; then allow to cool. Add to salmon along with green pepper and sour cream. Stir in chives and Tabasco. Arrange in hors d'oeuvre dish and sprinkle with chopped egg. *6 servings.*

Julienne of Vegetables

½ cup white part of
leeks, cut into
julienne strips
½ cup celery, cut
into julienne
strips
½ cup onions, cut
into julienne
strips
1 teaspoon salt
Freshly ground
pepper, to taste
½ cup olive oil
½ cup finely
chopped raw
mushrooms
½ cup mayonnaise

Place all ingredients except the mushrooms and mayonnaise in a saucepan
and simmer until the vegetables are
three-quarters cooked. Stir in mushrooms and cook until vegetables are
barely tender—they should be *al
dente*. Cool. Fold in mayonnaise;
taste for seasoning and correct if necessary. *8 servings.*

Red Cabbage Vinaigrette

1 small red
cabbage
1½ cups boiling
cider vinegar
4 tablespoons
olive oil
1 teaspoon salt
Freshly ground
pepper, to taste

Cut cabbage into fourths. Remove
heavy inner core. Shred cabbage very
finely, discarding any coarse strips
in evidence. Pour boiling water over
cabbage and let stand 5 minutes.
Drain well. Pour boiling vinegar over
drained cabbage and let stand 5 hours.
Drain very well and toss with remaining ingredients. Chill and serve.

Asparagus Spears in Dill Sauce

2 pounds fresh asparagus
1 teaspoon salt
½ pint commercial sour cream
2 tablespoons mayonnaise
2 tablespoons chopped fresh dill
½ teaspoon salt
¼ teaspoon freshly ground pepper
2 teaspoons lemon juice

Break off top 3 inches of asparagus spears only, saving the remainder for soup or such. Blanch asparagus by pouring boiling water over it, adding salt and simmering 5 minutes. Asparagus should be *al dente*. Mix sour cream, mayonnaise, dill, salt, pepper and lemon juice. Pour over well-drained, still-warm asparagus and toss well. Chill and serve.

Cauliflower in Mustard Sauce

1 head cauliflower
½ cup mayonnaise
1 tablespoon chopped capers
1 tablespoon chopped parsley
½ teaspoon salt
Freshly ground pepper, to taste
1 tablespoon prepared mustard

Cook cauliflower until barely tender; it should be *al dente*. Separate flowers into bite-size pieces. Mix mayonnaise with remaining ingredients and pour over warm cauliflower. Toss carefully together. Chill and serve.

CHAPTER 5

Salad in a Soup Bowl

Chilled Soups and Their Garnishes

One might
say I am stretching
a point in referring
to soups as salads.
However, there are
many fascinating
chilled soups that can
be considered salad fare;
& they are
wonderfully refreshing
for summer meals.

The creamed or heavier
cold soups, although not
salad-like, become
a supper main dish if served
with garlic bread
& followed by a
sumptuous dessert.
⟨Chilled soups
can be served in cups—
this is especially pleasant
on the terrace or patio
before dinner.
Some are best served in glasses rather than bowls or cups. All
cold soups should be taken from the refrigerator at the last
minute before serving. If using a tureen, chill it well before
pouring the soup into it. Jellied soups benefit greatly by being
presented with cup or bowl bedded in crushed ice.

There are many garnishes that can be used to glorify iced
soups. Garnish jellied soups with sprigs of watercress or parsley. Sprinkle finely chopped chives or scallions on creamed
soups. Cubes of bread fried in garlic-flavored butter do wonders for cold tomato soup or cold broths. Grated Parmesan
cheese tossed with parsley adds a piquant touch to bland
soups. A sophisticated garnish is a spoonful of salted whipped
cream on heavier creamed soups. Flute half a lemon, remove
the pulp, and fill it with sour cream or whipped cream and
float it on top of any cream-base soup. The garnishing possibilities are endless—don't be afraid to use your imagination.
Experiment with your own specialties and see what you arrive
at. Anything goes on a hot summer night.

BASIC CLEAR BROTHS

Broths are the foundation of many soups, both hot and cold.

Chicken Broth

1 fowl, 4 pounds or more	Clean fowl and remove as much fat as possible. Clean vegetables and cut into quarters. Place all in a large heavy kettle, add water to cover well, and add seasonings. Bring to a boil and skim off foam. Reduce heat and simmer for 3 hours. Remove chicken (make a chicken salad with the fowl), strain the broth and cool it. Place broth in the refrigerator overnight or until thoroughly cold. Remove the layer of fat. (This is an essential step.) Taste the broth. If it is too weak, place over high heat and reduce by boiling rapidly, uncovered, to desired strength. Pour through several thicknesses of dampened cheesecloth to remove all traces of sediment. When chilled, this broth jells beautifully and can be served in cups "as is," with a sprinkling of chopped parsley on top. It is the base of innumerable sauces and soups. *Makes about 1½ quarts.*
2 carrots	
2 onions	
2 sprigs celery with leaves	
3 or 4 sprigs parsley	
3 quarts water	
2 bay leaves	
5 or 6 peppercorns	
1 tablespoon salt	

Beef Broth

Follow the recipe above, replacing the fowl with 1 large, meaty soup bone, 1 pound of soup meat and 5 or 6 beef bouillon cubes.

Jellied Consommé Madrilène

1 can (4 ounces) tomato purée
1 quart Chicken Broth, page 99
Dash of cayenne
1 jar (4 ounces) pimientos, diced
Chopped parsley

Add tomato purée to the broth, bring to a boil, skim if necessary and reduce by boiling rapidly, uncovered, for 5 or 6 minutes. The total amount of liquid should be reduced by approximately 1 cup. Cool. Add the cayenne and diced pimiento. Chill thoroughly. Serve jellied, in cups, garnished with parsley. *8 servings.*

Jellied Celery Consommé

½ bunch celery, chopped with tops and leaves
6 cups Chicken Broth, page 99
Chopped parsley

Add celery to broth and bring to the boil. Cover and simmer 30 minutes. Strain through several thicknesses of dampened cheesecloth. Chill thoroughly. Serve in cups, sprinkled with chopped parsley. *8 servings.*

Consommé au Vin

¾ cup Madeira wine
or dry sherry
6 cups strong Chicken Broth, page 99
Chopped parsley

Add wine to warmed broth and stir well. Chill. Serve in cups, garnished with the parsley. *8 servings.*

Cream of Pea Soup with Mint

2 pounds fresh peas
2 stalks celery, including tops
1 cup boiling water
1 teaspoon salt
2 cups Chicken Broth, page 99
3 egg yolks
1 cup chopped fresh mint
½ cup diced cooked chicken
1 cup heavy cream

Shell peas and chop celery. Cook together in boiling salted water until tender. Drain and place in the blender with several tablespoons of chicken broth and purée. (If you do not have a blender, force vegetables through a fine sieve.) Add to the remaining broth and simmer for 10 minutes. Beat egg yolks. Add a small amount of the boiling liquid to the eggs, beating constantly; then, off the heat, gradually add the eggs to remaining soup. Return to heat and cook until thickened—do not boil. Add chopped mint. Cool, strain, add diced chicken and chill. Whip cream and fold into soup. Serve very cold. This soup is equally good served hot with croutons. *6 servings.*

Cold Cucumber Soup

A Balkan soup.

4 cups plain yogurt
2 cups diced
  cucumber
  Salt, to taste
  Freshly ground
  pepper, to taste
2 cloves garlic,
  crushed
2 tablespoons grated
  onion
  Chopped chives

Beat yogurt until smooth. Add cucumber, salt, pepper, garlic and onion. Chill thoroughly and serve surrounded by crushed ice. Sprinkle top of soup with chives. *8 servings.*

Potage Senegalese

3 sour apples,
  peeled, cored and
  sliced
1 large onion, sliced
1 tablespoon butter
2 teaspoons curry
  powder, or to taste
  Salt, to taste
  Freshly ground
  pepper, to taste
  Dash of cayenne
3 cups Chicken
  Broth, page 99

Sauté apples and onions in butter until soft; do not brown. Sprinkle with curry powder and cook 5 minutes, stirring constantly. Add salt and pepper and cayenne. Add broth and wine. Cook 10 minutes, stirring occasionally. Purée in blender, or force through a sieve. Return to a medium flame and bring to the boil. Beat egg yolks lightly. Add a few tablespoons of the boiling liquid to the egg yolks, stirring constantly. Off the heat, beat the egg mixture into the rest of the soup and

1 cup dry white
wine
3 egg yolks
1 cup heavy cream,
whipped
½ cup finely diced
cooked chicken
Paprika

reheat, being sure not to boil. When thickened remove from heat and chill. Fold in the whipped cream and the diced chicken. Sprinkle with paprika and serve ice cold. *8 servings.*

Iced Parsley Soup

1 large bunch pars-
ley, washed,
drained and
chopped
3 cups boiling
Chicken Broth,
page 99
2 egg yolks
2 cups light cream
½ teaspoon salt
Freshly ground
pepper, to taste
Worcestershire
sauce, to taste
Dairy sour cream
8 sprigs parsley

Reserve ¼ cup chopped parsley and add remainder to boiling broth. Simmer 20 minutes, then strain. Beat egg yolks and cream together. Gradually add about ½ cup hot liquid to the cream and egg mixture, then add this gradually to the hot soup off the heat, beating constantly with a wire whip. Heat over a low flame, stirring constantly, until soup will coat the back of a metal spoon. Do not allow to boil or the soup will curdle. Remove from heat and add salt, pepper and a few drops of Worcestershire sauce. Chill.

Stir ¼ cup chopped parsley into soup. Float a dollop of sour cream on the top of each cup of soup and place a sprig of parsley in the center of the cream. Serve ice cold. *8 servings.*

Vichyssoise

White part of 4 large leeks

1 medium onion

2 tablespoons butter

2 cups boiling Chicken Broth, page 99

3 medium potatoes, peeled and sliced

1 tablespoon salt

2 cups half-and-half (milk and cream)

Salt, to taste

White pepper, to taste

½ cup heavy cream, lightly whipped

Chopped chives

Cook finely sliced leeks and onions in butter until limp and golden—do not brown. Add broth, potatoes and salt. Cook 35 to 40 minutes, or until vegetables are very tender. Cool and purée in a blender or force through a sieve. Add half-and-half and white pepper and reheat. Correct seasoning and bring to a boil. Cook 2 to 3 minutes over a low flame. Cool, then chill thoroughly. Serve ice cold with a dollop of whipped cream and a sprinkling of chopped chives on each helping. 8 *servings*.

Cream of Watercress Soup

1 bunch watercress

Vichyssoise (*above*)

Watercress, for garnish

Cook cleaned bunch of watercress in boiling water for 2 to 3 minutes. Drain and purée in a blender, adding a few tablespoons of the vichyssoise to help make a smooth purée. Stir mixture into the vichyssoise and chill. Serve ice cold, garnished with a sprig of watercress in each helping. 8 *servings*.

Gazpacho

My husband brought this recipe back from Spain—you might say it is straight from the horse's mouth.

2 very large red tomatoes
2 medium green peppers
1 cucumber
½ cup bread crumbs
2 cups water
4 tablespoons olive oil
2 tablespoons wine vinegar
¼ teaspoon cayenne
2 cloves garlic, crushed
3 or 4 cumin seeds, crushed
1 teaspoon salt

Peel and chop the tomatoes, being sure not to lose any of the juice. Remove seeds from green peppers and chop. Peel cucumber and chop. Soak these vegetables and bread crumbs in the water for about half an hour. Add to this mixture the oil, vinegar, cayenne, garlic, cumin and salt. Place in a blender and purée. Pass through a fine sieve, removing all seeds. Chill thoroughly.

Serve in bowls. Pass small dishes of chopped cucumber, scallions, celery and chopped egg. Each diner adds his choice of these to his soup. *6 servings.*

Garnish:
1 cup chopped cucumber
1 cup chopped scallions
1 cup chopped celery
1 cup chopped hard-cooked eggs

Spanish Almond Soup

1½ cups blanched
almonds
1 teaspoon salt
2 cloves garlic,
crushed
½ cup olive oil
½ cup white wine
vinegar
1 tablespoon sugar
Dash of freshly
ground pepper
1 quart water
Seedless green
grapes, peeled

Purée all ingredients except the grapes in a blender. Strain through several layers of dampened cheesecloth. Chill thoroughly. Serve garnished with several green grapes. *6 servings.*

Ukrainian Borscht

This soup can be served hot or cold. If served cold, add 2 or 3 tablespoons of sugar to the soup and put a great dollop of sour cream in the center of each helping. The hot soup is delicious served with 1-inch lengths of frankfurter added. This recipe easily serves 12. Make the whole recipe and freeze any that is left over.

1 large onion
1½ pounds soup
meat
1 teaspoon salt
¼ teaspoon pepper
8 to 9 cups water

Cut onion into quarters and place it, along with meat, salt, pepper and water to cover, in a large kettle. Bring to a boil, skim and simmer 2 hours, or until meat is done. Strain stock, reserving meat. Place stock in refrig-

8 small beets
2 slices bacon
⅔ cup (or 1 small can) tomato paste
1 teaspoon vinegar
2 medium carrots
1 medium onion
1 stalk celery
2 tablespoons butter
2 tablespoons flour
½ small cabbage, cut into chunks
3 or 4 potatoes, peeled and quartered
1 bay leaf
2 teaspoons salt
1 clove garlic
Fresh dill or parsley
2 or 3 tablespoons sugar (optional)
Heavy dairy sour cream

erator overnight, then skim off and discard all fat. Add water, if necessary, to make 8 cups.

Peel beets, then slice in thin strips. Sauté bacon lightly, then add the beets and cook over medium heat for a few minutes, not allowing to brown. Add tomato paste and several tablespoons of the meat stock and cook over very low heat for 20 to 30 minutes. Stir occasionally, adding stock if necessary to prevent drying out. Remove from heat and add vinegar.

Chop carrots, onion and celery. Brown in 2 tablespoons butter. Sprinkle with flour, cook 2 or 3 minutes, then add, off the heat, 1 cup boiling stock. Set aside. Add beet mixture, cabbage and potatoes to remaining stock. Cook 10 to 15 minutes. Add browned vegetables, bay leaf and 2 teaspoons salt. Cook until all vegetables are soft. Cut meat into chunks and rub with the cut clove of garlic. Drop into the soup and reheat.

If soup is to be served cold, chill well, then sprinkle with dill or parsley and add sugar, if desired. Drop a spoonful of sour cream into the center of each soup bowl. *12 servings.*

Cold Schav

This was originally a Russian soup. It is now a beloved part of American Jewish cuisine. It is very refreshing on a hot summer day.

1 pound schav (*or sorrel or* sour grass)
2 onions, chopped
2 quarts water
2 teaspoons salt
1 tablespoon lemon juice
4 tablespoons sugar
Salt
Freshly ground pepper
2 egg yolks
2 hard-cooked eggs
1 cucumber, peeled and chopped
1 cup dairy sour cream

Clean the sour grass and shred it. Combine with onions, water and salt. Bring to a boil and simmer 45 minutes. Add lemon juice and sugar. Cook 10 minutes, then taste and add additional salt and pepper if necessary. Beat egg yolks and add a small amount of hot soup to them, beating constantly. Off heat, add this mixture to the body of the soup. Heat until thickened, but do not boil. Cool, then chill. Add chopped hard-cooked eggs and cucumber. Stir in sour cream. 8 *servings.*

COLD FRUIT SOUPS

Cold fruit soups are little served in America, much to our loss. They really shine as a patio appetizer, served in large handsome mugs a good 15 minutes before the meal. Europeans serve the sweeter soups as dessert, and if you are unconventional you can follow suit.

Danish Dried-Fruit Soup

½ pound mixed
  dried fruit
½ cup dried apples
¼ cup currants
¼ cup yellow raisins
1 teaspoon cinnamon
1 cup minute
  tapioca
¼ cup sugar
½ teaspoon salt
1 tablespoon grated
  lemon rind
½ cup heavy cream,
  whipped
  Slivered almonds
  (*optional*)

Place all fruits in water to cover and soak 8 hours or more. Add cinnamon. Bring to a boil, stirring, and simmer very slowly for 1½ hours. Stir often to prevent sticking. Add tapioca and cook 30 minutes more. Force through a sieve or whirl in a blender. Add sugar, salt and lemon rind. Stir until sugar dissolves. Chill. Serve with a dollop of whipped cream and a few slivered almonds, if desired. 8 *servings*.

Chilled Raspberry Soup

3½ cups raspberries
3½ cups water
¾ cup sweet red wine
Dash of salt
¾ cup sugar (or less, depending on sweetness of wine)
1 cup dairy sour cream

Reserve about 6 or 8 large berries. Mash remaining raspberries and force through a fine sieve. Add water, wine, salt and sugar to pulp. Bring to a boil and simmer, tightly covered, for 5 minutes. Cool. Add ¾ cup sour cream and stir until thoroughly incorporated. Chill and serve in cups, garnished with remaining sour cream. Float a berry on top of the cream. *6 to 8 servings.*

Russian Apple Soup

This is much like a thin applesauce. It can be served as a dessert soup or as a refreshing between-meals snack.

6 tart green apples
1 cup sugar
4 cups water
½ teaspoon cinnamon
1 teaspoon vanilla

Peel apples and dice. Combine with sugar and allow to stand 30 minutes. Bring water to a boil, then add apples and cinnamon. Simmer until soft. Force through a sieve, or whirl in the blender. Add vanilla and chill. *8 servings.*

Cold Strawberry Soup

This is a rich and beautiful soup that tastes almost like melted ice cream, except for its greater tartness. My advice is to serve small portions.

2 quarts strawberries, hulled and washed
Juice of 2 lemons
3 cloves
1 bay leaf
Pinch of mace
Pinch of marjoram
4 cups water
⅓ cup sugar
2 tablespoons cornstarch
1 cup dairy sour cream

Cook berries, lemon juice, cloves, bay leaf, mace, marjoram and water together for 15 minutes. Remove from heat and cool. Purée in blender, then strain through a fine sieve. Return to heat, stir in sugar and bring to a boil. Dissolve the cornstarch in a little water; then gradually add to the soup, stirring constantly. When thickened and clear, remove from heat and cool, then chill. Before serving, fold in the sour cream, reserving a small amount for a garnish. Present in bowls, garnished with a dollop of sour cream topped with a whole strawberry. *8 to 10 servings.*

CHAPTER 6

Vegetables Vinaigrette
Vegetables Dressed for the Salad

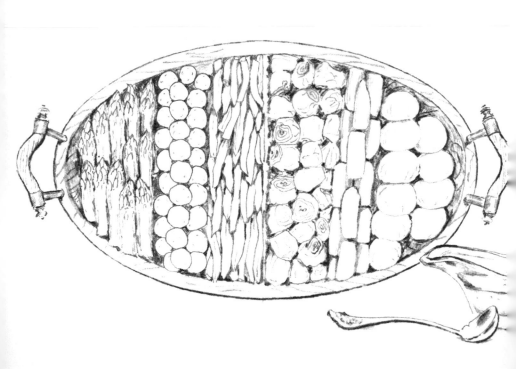

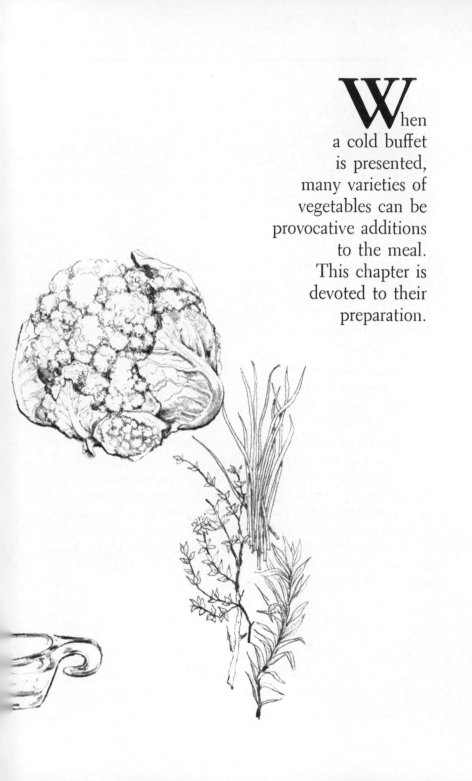

When
a cold buffet
is presented,
many varieties of
vegetables can be
provocative additions
to the meal.
This chapter is
devoted to their
preparation.

You will find
many ways to use
leftover vegetables
that will entrance you.
Most of the following
recipes can be adapted
to vegetables
previously cooked
by steaming, baking or
boiling, &
I strongly advise
experimentation
on your part.

The term "vinaigrette" refers to the dressing of any food with a vinaigrette dressing, often called "French dressing." I use it loosely for the heading of this chapter; some recipes call for other methods.

Vegetables prepared with a vinaigrette dressing may be presented as part of a large salad platter or as a separate dish. Many may be served as a main-course accompaniment: merely arrange dressed vegetables on a lettuce leaf and serve garnished with sliced tomato, a scallion, green olives or a wedge of hard-cooked egg.

The first recipe given below is a marinade in which most raw vegetables can be cooked, then chilled and drained. They may accompany any buffet fare.

Vegetables à la Grecque

This is the basic à la grecque recipe referred to throughout the book.

4 cups of raw
vegetables of
your choice, such
as mushrooms,
carrots, cauli-
flower, etc.,
cleaned and cut

Marinade:
4 cups water
Juice of 4 lemons
1 cup olive oil
1 teaspoon salt
¼ teaspoon freshly
  ground pepper
3 coriander seeds
  Pinch of thyme
1 bay leaf
1 stalk fennel
1 stalk celery

Place vegetables in saucepan. Mix remaining ingredients together and pour over the vegetables. Bring to a boil and simmer, covered, until the vegetable is barely cooked. It should have a texture slightly resistant to the bite, or verging on crispness—*al dente*, as the Italians term it. Remove from heat, cool and chill in marinade. Just before serving drain well and serve as desired. The marinade can be reserved and used again for another vegetable; if refrigerated it will keep for several weeks. *Makes 5 cups marinade; 8 servings of vegetable.*

Artichoke Hearts

8 artichokes
  Boiling water
1 teaspoon salt

Remove any tough outer leaves. Trim off stems and cut off tips of leaves. Tie each artichoke and stand in a large pot on a rack. Pour boiling water into the bottom of the pot to a depth of about 2 inches. Add salt and cook, tightly covered, for approximately 45 minutes, or until a leaf pulls out easily. Drop at once into cold water. Remove leaves and scoop out the choke. Dress hearts as desired. *8 servings.*

Artichoke Hearts Vinaigrette

8 artichoke hearts,
  cooked as directed
  in preceding
  recipe
3 tablespoons olive
  oil
1 tablespoon wine
  vinegar
½ teaspoon salt
  Pinch of dry
  mustard
  Freshly ground
  pepper, to taste

Place artichoke hearts in a bowl. Beat together remaining ingredients, pour over hearts and marinate for several hours. Serve on lettuce leaves, toss in a green salad or serve as desired. *8 servings.*

Artichoke Hearts à la Grecque

2 boxes (9 ounces) frozen artichoke hearts
¼ recipe Marinade for Vegetables à la Grecque, page 115

Cook artichoke hearts in marinade as directed. Chill in marinade and serve as an appetizer, or drain and add to a salad. *8 servings.*

Artichokes with Sauce Tartare

Dress cooked artichoke hearts with English Mayonnaise, page 48, adding 2 tablespoons chopped chives to the dressing.

Asparagus Spears Vinaigrette

3 pounds asparagus, cooked, *or* 2 packages frozen asparagus spears, cooked
½ recipe Lemon French Dressing, page 46
1 hard-cooked egg yolk, chopped Lettuce, washed and crisped

Marinate asparagus spears in dressing for at least 2 hours. Drain and arrange on lettuce leaves. Sprinkle with the chopped egg yolk. *8 servings.*

Eggplant à la Grecque

2 large eggplants
Marinade for
Vegetables à la
Grecque, page 115

Peel eggplant and cut into 1-inch cubes. Bring marinade to a boil and add eggplant cubes gradually. Simmer 12 to 15 minutes, cool in marinade and serve as an appetizer; or drain and serve on an antipasto platter. *8 servings.*

Green-Bean Salad Vinaigrette

2 pounds whole
green beans,
freshly cooked, *or*
2 packages (10
ounces) frozen
French-style green
beans, cooked
Basic French Dress-
ing, page 44
1 tablespoon
chopped chives
1 tablespoon
chopped parsley
1 Spanish onion,
sliced thin

While beans are still warm pour dressing over them and allow to cool. Arrange on lettuce leaves and sprinkle with herbs. Surround with onion slices. *8 servings.*

Bean Salad

2 cups cooked green
beans
1 can (1 pound)
kidney beans,
drained
1 can (1 pound)
black-eyed peas,
drained
1 green pepper, sliced
in rings
1 onion, sliced and
separated into rings
Dressing (below)
Romaine lettuce,
washed and crisped

Place beans, black-eyed peas, pepper and onion rings in bowl. Pour dressing over vegetables and marinate overnight in refrigerator. Arrange on a bed of romaine. *10 to 12 servings.*

Dressing:

¾ cup salad oil
¼ cup wine vinegar
¼ cup sugar
1 teaspoon salt
½ teaspoon dry
mustard
½ teaspoon dried
tarragon
½ teaspoon dried
basil
2 tablespoons
chopped parsley

Beat or shake all ingredients together until well blended.

White Bean Salad

3 cups cooked and
  drained white
  beans
4 scallions, chopped,
  green tops and all
1 jar (4 ounces)
  pimientos, drained
  and diced
  Boiled Dressing I,
  page 50
  Lettuce leaves,
  washed and crisped
2 hard-cooked eggs,
  chopped fine

Place beans, scallions and pimientos in a bowl. Toss lightly with salad dressing. Arrange on lettuce leaves and sprinkle with chopped egg. 8 *servings.*

Beets Vinaigrette

3 cups cooked beets
  cut into thin
  julienne strips
  Basic French Dress-
  ing, page 45, with
  onion variation
1 hard-cooked egg,
  chopped fine
  Lettuce, washed
  and crisped

Toss first three ingredients well together and serve on lettuce leaves. 8 *servings.*

Pickled Beets

These beets will keep indefinitely if refrigerated.

½ cup cider vinegar
½ cup cooking liquid
from beets
3 tablespoons sugar
½ teaspoon salt
Freshly ground
pepper, to taste
½ teaspoon dry mustard
1 teaspoon celery
seed
3 cups sliced cooked
beets

Bring all ingredients but the celery seed and beets to a boil. Sprinkle celery seed over beets, pour boiling liquid over them and place in a jar. Serve as a garnish for salad plates or as a relish. *Enough to garnish 12 salad servings.*

Stuffed Cabbage Leaves

A good addition to the hors d'oeuvre tray.

2 cups boiled rice
½ cup grated Parmesan cheese
2 tablespoons
melted butter
16 cabbage leaves,
blanched in boiling water for 5
minutes
Marinade for
Vegetables à la
Grecque, page
115

Mix rice, cheese and butter. Place a small mound in the center of each cabbage leaf, fold in ends and roll up. Skewer with toothpicks. Place rolls in marinade and braise about 10 minutes. Remove from marinade. Strain liquid over cabbage rolls, cool them, then chill. Remove toothpicks and serve. *8 servings.*

Cole Slaw with Sour-Cream Dressing

1 large head cabbage
1 teaspoon dill seed
¼ cup chopped parsley
Dressing (*below*)

Cut cabbage into quarters, remove core and shred very fine with a sharp knife. Remove any coarse pieces. Toss with the dill seed and parsley. Add dressing and refrigerate until needed. *8 servings.*

Dressing:

4 eggs
1 teaspoon sugar
1 teaspoon salt
Freshly ground pepper, to taste
½ teaspoon dry mustard
½ cup oil
3 tablespoons vinegar
½ cup dairy sour cream

Beat eggs well and add sugar, salt, pepper and mustard. Place over simmering water and cook, stirring, until thickened. (Stir vigorously, as the eggs must not scramble. If they tend to lump nevertheless, force through a sieve or whirl in blender.) Remove from heat and very gradually beat in the oil and vinegar. Cool, then fold in the sour cream.

Carrots à la Grecque

1 bunch carrots
½ recipe Marinade for Vegetables à la Grecque, page 115

Scrape and cut carrots into thin julienne strips. Bring marinade to the boil and drop carrots into it. Cook until barely tender. Drain, cool and serve as a component of a complete-meal salad. *6 servings.*

Cauliflower à la Grecque

1 head cauliflower
Marinade for Vegetables à la Grecque, page 115

Wash and remove green stalk from cauliflower. Separate head into small florets. Cook in marinade until barely tender; it *must not be over-cooked.* Cool and serve as an appetizer or as a garnish on a buffet platter. *6 servings.*

Cauliflower Vinaigrette

1 head cauliflower, cooked whole just until tender
Basic French Dressing, page 44
1 tablespoon chopped parsley

Separate cooked cauliflower into florets. Pour dressing over cauliflower, preferably while it is still warm. Cool, then chill in marinade. Sprinkle with parsley. *6 servings.*

Stuffed Celery or Chinese Cabbage I

1 bunch celery *or* Chinese cabbage
1 package (8 ounces) cream cheese
3 tablespoons chives *or* scallions, chopped
Paprika

Choose large firm heads of celery or Chinese cabbage and clean carefully. Cut into 3-inch lengths. Mash cream cheese with a fork to soften, then add the chopped chives or scallions. Force into the celery or cabbage sections. (You can use a pastry bag for this if you are proficient.) Sprinkle with paprika and serve as an appetizer or as a relish on the buffet table. *12 servings.*

Stuffed Celery or Chinese Cabbage II

1 bunch celery *or* Chinese cabbage
1 pound cooked, shelled and deveined shrimp
½ cup mayonnaise
1 teaspoon salt
Dash of pepper
Capers

Clean and cut stalks of celery or Chinese cabbage into 3-inch lengths. Chop shrimp very fine, then mash with a fork. Fold in mayonnaise and add salt and pepper. Force into celery or cabbage sections. Garnish with capers and serve as an appetizer. *12 servings.*

Cucumber Relish

2 large cucumbers, peeled and diced
1½ cups water
½ cup salad oil
Juice of 1 lemon
Bouquet garni consisting of a sprig of celery, pinch of dried thyme, 1 bay leaf, pinch of ground coriander (*see* page 259)
½ teaspoon salt
Freshly ground pepper, to taste

Boil all together 3 to 4 minutes. Drain cucumber, reserving liquid; discard *bouquet garni*. Boil liquid down by half. Pour over cucumber and chill. *8 servings.*

Anne's Greek Cucumber Salad

4 cucumbers
6 tablespoons olive oil
2 tablespoons tarragon vinegar
½ teaspoon salt
Freshly ground pepper, to taste
1 cup dairy sour cream

Peel cucumbers and slice very thin. Marinate in oil, vinegar, salt and pepper for several hours. Just before serving fold in the sour cream. *8 servings.*

Italian Eggplant

2 medium eggplants
½ cup olive oil
2 onions, sliced
1 No. 2 can tomatoes
2 stalks celery, diced
1 bottle (2¼ ounces) capers
2 tablespoons sugar
4 tablespoons wine vinegar
Salt, to taste
Freshly ground pepper, to taste

Peel and dice eggplants. Sauté in hot oil until lightly browned. Drain on paper toweling and place in a large skillet. Fry onions in remaining oil until golden. Add tomatoes and celery and simmer until tender. Stir in drained capers. Fold into eggplant. Place sugar, vinegar, salt and pepper in a small saucepan and heat until sugar dissolves. Pour over eggplant mixture and simmer, covered, about 20 minutes. Cool thoroughly before serving. 8 servings.

Mushrooms à la Grecque

1 pound button mushrooms
½ recipe Marinade for Vegetables à la Grecque, page 115

Place cleaned, unpeeled small white button mushrooms in a saucepan with marinade. Simmer, covered, until mushrooms are barely tender, approximately 15 minutes. Cool and serve in marinade. 6 servings.

Boiled Onions Stuffed with Eggs

8 medium-size
white onions
4 hard-cooked eggs
½ cup mayonnaise or
boiled dressing
Salt, to taste
Freshly ground
pepper, to taste
2 tablespoons
chopped parsley

Peel onions and drop into boiling salted water. Boil until tender when pierced—approximately 35 to 40 minutes. Cool. Gently force center sections of onion out, leaving a ¼-inch shell. Chop centers of onion very fine along with the hard-cooked eggs. Bind with the mayonnaise or dressing, add seasonings and parsley. Carefully fill onion shells, mounding filling up slightly. *8 servings.*

Hungarian Green Peppers

4 green peppers
3 tablespoons wine
vinegar
½ teaspoon salt
Freshly ground
pepper, to taste
2 tablespoons oil
½ teaspoon sugar

Preheat oven to 350° F. Wash and dry green peppers. Place in oven for 10 to 15 minutes, or until skin blisters. Remove from oven and peel off the thin outer skin. Cut stem ends off and remove seeds, being careful not to puncture flesh. Cut into rings. Marinate in dressing made with remaining ingredients. *6 to 8 servings.*

Green Peppers in Vinegar

5 green peppers
1 teaspoon allspice
4 or 5 sprigs fresh
   thyme
1 clove garlic
1 tablespoon salt
2 cups cider vinegar

Halve and seed the green peppers. Place in a 1-quart jar and add allspice, thyme, garlic and salt. Fill jar with vinegar, seal and store for 2 to 3 months. Use thinly sliced in salads.

French Potato Salad

6 medium potatoes
3 tablespoons
   chopped parsley
3 scallions, chopped
1 cup Basic French
   Dressing, page 44
   Salt, to taste
   Freshly ground
   pepper, to taste
   Paprika

Peel potatoes and cook in boiling salted water until barely tender. Drain and slice. Add parsley and scallions, and while still warm pour the dressing over all. Add salt and pepper. Cool to room temperature. Just before serving sprinkle with paprika. 8 *servings.*

Potato Salad with Champagne

This recipe can be made with 2 cups of dry white wine as a substitute for the champagne.

4 medium potatoes
4 hard-cooked eggs
1 can (2 ounces) anchovy fillets
1 jar (5 ounces) pickled herring
1½ pounds cooked, shelled and deveined shrimp
2 cups cooked green beans
1 small bottle champagne
¼ cup brandy
¾ cup Lemon French Dressing, page 46
Stuffed green olives

Peel potatoes and cook until barely tender in boiling salted water. Slice ⅛ inch thick. Slice eggs. Drain and chop anchovies. Cut herring into bite-size pieces. While potatoes are still warm arrange in a bowl alternate layers of potatoes, shrimp, beans, eggs, anchovies and herring, repeating until all ingredients are used. Pour enough champagne over all to barely cover. Marinate 3 hours. Just before serving toss with brandy and French dressing. Garnish with olives. *8 to 10 servings.*

American Potato Salad

6 medium potatoes
3 tablespoons chopped parsley
1 onion, finely chopped
¼ cup vermouth
¾ cup mayonnaise
Salt, to taste
Freshly ground pepper, to taste
1 tablespoon celery seed
Paprika

Peel potatoes and cook in boiling salted water. When barely tender, drain and cool. Slice potatoes and add parsley and chopped onion. Mix vermouth and mayonnaise and beat until well blended. Toss with potato mixture. Add celery seed and salt and pepper. Toss again and garnish with paprika. *8 servings.*

Marinated Sweet Potatoes or Yams

2 large sweet potatoes *or* yams
½ cup olive *or* other salad oil
¼ cup vinegar
2 tablespoons honey
½ teaspoon salt
¼ cup water
Freshly ground pepper, to taste

Peel sweet potatoes or yams and cut in very thin strips 2 to 3 inches long. Place in a saucepan with the remaining ingredients and cook uncovered approximately 15 minutes, or until barely cooked: the strips should be still slightly resistant to the bite. Chill in the cooking liquid and serve. *6 servings.*

Beefsteak-Tomato Salad

4 large, very red beefsteak tomatoes
1 tablespoon sugar, preferably the superfine type
4 tablespoons olive oil
1 tablespoon wine vinegar
½ teaspoon salt
Freshly ground pepper, to taste
1 tablespoon chopped fresh tarragon, or ½ teaspoon dried tarragon

Slice tomatoes and sprinkle with sugar. Mix oil, vinegar and salt and pepper. Pour over tomatoes. Sprinkle with tarragon. Chill. *8 servings.*

Zucchini à la Grecque

1 pound zucchini
2 cups Marinade for Vegetables à la Grecque, page 115
1 teaspoon oregano

Scrub zucchini well, slice ¼ inch thick and cook in marinade until barely tender. Sprinkle with oregano and chill. *8 servings.*

CHAPTER 7

The Shape of Salads
to Come

Aspics and Other Molded Salads

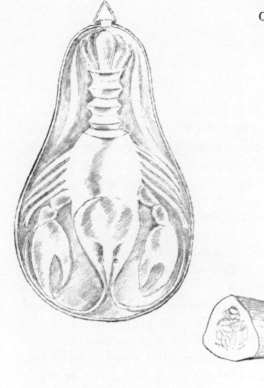

Under
the heading
of molded salads
there are two
main categories:
salads with a gelatin base
& those based on a
natural meat, poultry
or fish jelly, or aspic.

The gelatin salad
is made
with unflavored
gelatin powder,
with various added
ingredients.
When chilled, gelatin
salads have a firm
jelly-like consistency.
They can be unmolded
& will retain
their shape
when standing free.

Aspics are based on the jelly formed by chilling a strong broth made from the bones and trimmings of fish, fowl or meat. They, too, can be unmolded. Savory aspics may also be made with a clear broth or vegetable juice to which unflavored gelatin is added.

Many molded salads are sweet, whereas aspics are not. Aspics are always used in conjunction with fish, fowl, meat or vegetables. The gelatin salad usually contains fruits or vegetables. Both are served on the buffet table, and both can be elegant luncheon main dishes.

There are countless other varieties of jellied dishes. Of these the galantine is perhaps the most glamorous. This is a whole fowl, boned, stuffed, poached and encased in aspic. Head cheese (a misleading term in that there is no cheese involved) is made by simmering the head of a calf or pig in a well-seasoned broth, stripping the meat from the bones and chilling the meat in the strained broth, which jells firmly. A classic Jewish dish is a lovely calf's-foot jelly called *pitcha* or *sulze*. (All these recipes follow.) There are so many recipes in this category that I can only skim the surface and offer those that I enjoy the most.

There are a few rules to follow to produce attractive aspics and molded salads. The mold should always be rinsed in cold water and chilled before filling. This helps the salad to unmold more satisfactorily; the liquid mixture will adhere to the mold upon contact and immediately begin to set.

If you wish to line a mold with clear gelatin or aspic, put a small amount of the mixture into a very cold mold and swirl it quickly around until a thin layer coats the surface. Refrigerate the mold until the lining has thoroughly jelled, then repeat the process as many times as necessary to obtain a lining of the thickness desired. This is referred to as "layering." If the supply of gelatin or aspic tends to set between bouts of layering, heat it gently until it melts, or keep it over warm water until finished. Aspic is also used to coat certain prepared fish or meat dishes. It is allowed to set between layers until the coating is as thick as desired. The food enclosed in aspic is then trimmed of any excess that has accumulated in the dish; this jelly is chopped and used as a garnish.

If you should find that your broth is not making a firm enough jelly, heat the broth, soften one envelope of unflavored gelatin in a little cold water and add to the hot broth, stirring until dissolved. Allow to cool before using.

Aspic should always be clarified before use, as directed in the following recipes. This is most important in ensuring the clear beauty of your finished dish.

A word on the unmolding of aspics and gelatins: The easiest method is to dip the mold quickly into a basin of very hot water, being sure the water does not spill into the mold. Hold the mold in the water for a few seconds—only just long enough to melt the contents very slightly. Quickly invert a platter over the mold and turn platter and mold together, with the mold centered on the platter, and lift the mold from the salad.

Another method is to invert the mold on the platter and cover it with a towel wrung out of very hot water. This method is not as quick and sure as the first, but has the advantage of permitting the platter to be decorated before the salad is unmolded.

ASPICS

Basic Beef Aspic

¼ pound salt pork, cubed

2 large carrots

2 onions

3 leeks

3 stalks celery

2 pounds lean stewing beef

1 pound meaty veal knuckles

1 or 2 calf's feet
Boiling water
Herb bouquet consisting of bay leaf, parsley, thyme and celery leaves

1 tablespoon salt

½ teaspoon freshly ground pepper

3 egg whites, slightly beaten

½ pound very lean beef, ground

1 teaspoon dried tarragon

Place cubed salt pork in a large heavy-bottomed pot and, over very low heat, render the fat from the pork. Discard remaining pork. Dice the carrots, onions, leeks and celery. Brown the vegetables, along with the beef, veal and calf's feet, in the rendered pork fat. Cover the browned ingredients with boiling water and add the herb bouquet, salt and freshly ground pepper. Bring to a boil, skim thoroughly and simmer for 5 to 6 hours. Strain and cool. Skim off as much fat as possible and discard.

To clarify: Place slightly beaten egg whites, ground lean beef and tarragon in a flat-bottomed pot. Pour in the cool broth and stir vigorously. Bring to a boil, stirring constantly, lower heat and simmer 35 minutes. Strain through several layers of cheesecloth wrung out of cold water. Chill. Remove any traces of fat. *10 to 12 cups broth.*

Basic Chicken Aspic

Follow preceding recipe, substituting 1 large fowl, cut up, for the stewing beef. Omit ground meat when clarifying.

Fish Aspic or Stock

This recipe makes excellent fish stock when gelatin, egg white and eggshells are omitted.

3 pounds fish heads, bones, tails and fins, washed
1 onion, peeled and quartered
½ cup chopped parsley
Juice of ½ lemon
½ teaspoon thyme
1 bay leaf
1 teaspoon salt
5 peppercorns
1 celery top with leaves
1 cup dry white wine
2 envelopes (2 tablespoons) unflavored gelatin
1 egg white, slightly beaten
1 eggshell, crushed

Place fish trimmings, onion, parsley, lemon juice, thyme, bay leaf, salt, peppercorns and celery leaves in a large heavy-bottomed pot. Add enough water to barely cover. Bring to the boil and skim top to remove any scum that accumulates. Add wine and simmer 30 minutes. Cool and strain through 2 thicknesses of cheesecloth wrung out in cold water.

Sprinkle gelatin over stock and return to heat. Bring to the simmering point. Add the beaten egg white and eggshell. Simmer very gently for 15 minutes. Do not boil.

Remove from heat and allow to cool. Strain through 2 thicknesses of dampened cheesecloth. *Yields approximately 1½ quarts aspic.*

Quick Aspic

3 cups Chicken
Broth (page 99),
Beef Broth (page
100), or bottled
clam juice
1 cup tomato juice
4 envelopes (4
tablespoons) un-
flavored gelatin
Salt, to taste
Freshly ground
pepper, to taste
1 teaspoon sugar
2 egg whites, slightly
beaten
2 eggshells, crushed
¼ cup sherry

Place all ingredients except sherry in a saucepan and bring to a boil, stirring constantly. Stir in sherry; then strain through several thicknesses of cheesecloth wrung out in cold water. Yield, 4½ cups.

Quick Wine Aspic

3 cups Chicken
Broth (page 99)
1 cup dry white wine
4 envelopes unfla-
vored gelatin
Salt and pepper to
taste
2 egg whites, slightly
beaten
2 eggshells, crushed

Place all ingredients in a saucepan and bring to a boil, stirring constantly. Remove from heat and strain through several thicknesses of damp cheesecloth. Yield, about 4 cups.

Chicken with Tarragon in Aspic

4½ pound roasting
chicken
8 cups Chicken
Broth, page 99
2 teaspoons dried
tarragon
½ pound very lean
beef, ground
1 egg white,
slightly beaten
2 envelopes (2
tablespoons) un-
flavored gelatin
¼ cup cold water
½ cup Madeira
wine
Fresh tarragon *or*
mint leaves
Sprigs of water-
cress *or* parsley

Clean chicken and truss. Put into a deep pot and cover with chicken broth, using more if necessary. Add 1 teaspoon dried tarragon. Cook 1 hour, or until bird is tender. Allow to cool, uncovered, in broth. Remove and drain chicken. Refrigerate until needed. Place broth in refrigerator until fat coagulates, then remove all fat.

Place broth in a saucepan and add the lean beef, the remaining 1 tea-spoon tarragon and the beaten egg white. Bring to a boil, stirring; sim-mer 25 minutes, then strain through several layers of cheesecloth wrung out in cold water. Soften gelatin in ¼ cup cold water. Add to strained broth. Add wine. Select an oval plat-ter large enough to accommodate the chicken. Pour a thin layer of aspic over the bottom and chill until firm.

Untruss chilled chicken and place on bed of aspic. Spoon a layer of aspic over the chicken and allow to set. Ar-range fresh tarragon or mint leaves over chicken breast and carefully spoon on another layer of aspic to hold the garnish in place. Chill until set. Repeat coating process until there is as thick a layer of aspic as desired. Trim excess aspic from around sides of chicken, chop up and return to platter, surrounding chicken closely. Garnish with watercress or parsley. *4 to 6 servings.*

Classic Tomato Aspic

1¾ cups tomato juice
3 tablespoons minced onion
2 tablespoons minced celery
1 tablespoon brown sugar
½ teaspoon salt
1 small bay leaf, crumbled
2 whole cloves
1 envelope (1 tablespoon) unflavored gelatin
¼ cup cold water
Juice of 1 lemon

Place tomato juice, onion, celery, brown sugar, salt and spices in saucepan and boil 5 minutes. Strain. Soften gelatin in cold water, then dissolve in hot mixture. Add lemon juice. Pour into a rinsed 1-quart mold or 6 rinsed individual molds. Chill until firm and unmold. *6 servings.*

Eggs in Aspic with Ham

This can be served as a supper dish, as an appetizer or on the buffet.

1 recipe Chicken Aspic, page 138, *or* Quick Aspic made with chicken broth, page 139
8 thin slices truffle, *or* 8 carrot flowers *or* other garnish of your choice
8 cold, firmly poached eggs
8 thin slices cooked ham

Rinse 8 individual molds with cold water and chill thoroughly. Spoon a layer of aspic into each and allow to set. Arrange a slice of truffle or a carrot flower or other garnish in each mold, spoon aspic over it and allow to set. Trim eggs to fit molds and place an egg in each mold. Pour in aspic until mold is filled. Chill until firmly set. Trim ham slices to size of molds. Unmold eggs onto ham. Pour a thin coating of aspic over both to secure aspic mold to ham. Chill. Trim each mold as needed and arrange on a platter, surrounded with chopped leftover aspic. *8 servings.*

Stuffed Ham in Aspic

1 3- to 4-pound boneless ham
4 to 6 cups water
½ lemon, sliced
1 bay leaf
1 onion
5 or 6 peppercorns

Place ham, water, lemon, bay leaf, onion and peppercorns in a large kettle and simmer 2 to 3 hours, or until ham is tender. Cool, uncovered, in liquid. Remove ham and slice lengthwise ¼ inch thick. Reshape ham and set aside.

½ pound liverwurst
2 tablespoons mayonnaise
2 tablespoons chopped parsley
½ teaspoon salt
Freshly ground pepper, to taste
1½ cups Chicken Broth, page 99
½ cup tomato juice
2 envelopes (2 tablespoons) unflavored gelatin
2 egg whites, slightly beaten
2 crushed eggshells
2 tablespoons Marsala wine
1 jar (4 ounces) pimientos, *or*
1 hard-cooked egg

Filling: Mash together to a smooth paste the liverwurst, mayonnaise, chopped parsley, salt and pepper to taste. Spread between ham slices, reserving enough to cover top and sides of ham. Reconstruct ham and spread with remaining liver paste. Chill thoroughly.

Aspic: Combine chicken broth, tomato juice, gelatin, beaten egg whites and eggshells in a saucepan and bring just to a boil, stirring constantly. Remove from heat. Strain through several layers of cheesecloth wrung out in cold water. Stir in wine.

When ham is thoroughly chilled, spoon a layer of aspic over it. Allow to set. This takes a very short time, as the aspic is very thick. If aspic sets before use, reheat slowly until melted.

Cut strips of pimiento or circles of hard-cooked egg, or both, and decorate top of ham. Spoon another layer of aspic over the ham and the garnish. Allow to set. Repeat process of layering with aspic until desired effect is achieved. Trim excess aspic from around ham and chop it. Place ham on a large handsome carving board, surround with chopped aspic, and cut in very thin crosswise slices to serve. *10 to 12 servings.*

Ham and Parsley Aspic

2 calf's feet
Soup bone with meat (2 pounds)
Several sprigs parsley
2 or 3 stalks celery, with leaves
1 large onion, chopped
2 bay leaves
4 or 5 peppercorns
1 teaspoon dried thyme
½ bottle dry white wine
7 pounds of ham, bone in
2 egg whites, slightly beaten
1 envelope (1 tablespoon) unflavored gelatin
½ cup water
¼ cup dry white wine
1 tablespoon wine vinegar
1 cup chopped parsley

Place calf's feet, soup bone, parsley, celery, onion, bay leaves, peppercorns, thyme and ½ bottle wine in a large kettle and cover with water. Simmer 2 hours, then add ham. Simmer until ham is tender. Remove ham from bone, chop fine and set aside. Strain stock through a sieve and refrigerate. Remove fat and discard. Add egg whites to cold stock. Heat very slowly, stirring until boiling point is reached. Soften gelatin in ½ cup water, add to broth and stir until dissolved. Strain through several layers of cheesecloth wrung out in cold water. Add wine and vinegar.

Toss ham with parsley until well mixed. Pack into a 2-quart mold which has been lightly oiled. Pour aspic over ham until mold is full. Chill until firm, then unmold on a platter. *12 servings.*

Fillets of Sole in Aspic

6 large fillets of sole
Juice of 1 lemon
Freshly ground
pepper, to taste
1 cup bottled clam
juice
1 cup dry white wine
Quick Aspic, using
bottled clam juice,
page 139
Large stuffed green
olives
3 cups American
Potato Salad, page
145

Sprinkle sole with lemon juice and freshly ground pepper. Roll up in jelly-roll fashion and skewer with toothpicks. Heat clam juice and wine together in a saucepan and add fish rolls. Poach, barely simmering, for 12 to 15 minutes. Remove fish rolls, cool and chill thoroughly. Strain poaching liquid and use with additional clam juice, if needed, to make the Quick Aspic.

When fish rolls are thoroughly chilled, slice ½ inch thick. Place a slice of stuffed olive in the center of each slice, making a spiral of fish with a center of green. Secure olive by spooning aspic over each fish slice. Rinse a 2-quart ring mold in cold water, then chill in the refrigerator. Coat the bottom and sides by swirling aspic around in the very cold mold—it should firm up almost immediately. Dip each roll in aspic and arrange around the sides and on the bottom of the mold, with the olive garnish facing the outside. (If remaining aspic tends to jell before you are finished, heat gently to dissolve.) Spoon in a little more aspic to hold slices in place. Allow to set, then fill mold with remaining aspic. Chill until firm. If there is any aspic left, al-

low to set in a shallow platter.
Chill the potato salad. Unmold
fish aspic on a platter and garnish
with lettuce. Fill center with potato
salad. Chop remaining aspic, if any,
and encircle mold with it. 8 *servings.*

Shrimp Mousse in Aspic

2 tablespoons
butter
2 small carrots,
diced
½ cup chopped
onion
¼ cup chopped
celery
1 cup chopped raw
ham
½ teaspoon thyme
or few sprigs of
fresh thyme
½ bay leaf
1 cup dry white
wine
1 teaspoon salt
¼ teaspoon freshly
ground pepper
3 pounds raw
shrimp, peeled
and deveined

Melt 2 tablespoons butter in a saucepan and add carrots, onions, celery
and ham. Toss well with butter and
cook until vegetables are barely tender. Add thyme, bay leaf, wine, salt
and pepper to taste. Bring to a
boil and add shrimp. Cook only until
shrimp turn pink. Remove enough
shrimp to decorate mold, about a
quarter of the 3 pounds. Remove bay
leaf and thyme stalks, if any. Scrape
the remaining shrimp, liquid and
vegetables into the blender and purée. (If you do not have a blender,
put through a food mill, or force
through a sieve.) Add the Velouté
Sauce to this mixture. Fold in
whipped cream and correct seasoning
if necessary.

Rinse a fish-shaped mold in cold
water, then chill. Arrange the reserved shrimp decoratively in the

½ cup Velouté Sauce, page 73
1¼ cups heavy cream, whipped
Salt, to taste
Freshly ground pepper, to taste
Sliced truffles *or* strips of pimiento
2 cups Fish Aspic, page 138
Lettuce

mold along with the pimiento or truffles. Pour a thin layer of aspic over the garnish to hold it in place. Allow to set and repeat the process, tipping the mold, to allow a shell of aspic to set completely around the sides. When firm, press the shrimp mousse into the shell and pour a layer of aspic over the top. Chill until set. Unmold on a bed of lettuce. *6 to 8 servings.*

Turkey Slices in Aspic

2 cans (4½ ounces each) deviled ham
4 teaspoons prepared horseradish
2 tablespoons chopped parsley
1 onion, grated
12 slices turkey breast
6 hard-cooked eggs
Pitted black olives
2 cups Quick Aspic made with chicken broth, page 139
Lettuce

Mash deviled ham and mix with horseradish, parsley and grated onion. Trim slices of turkey into uniform ovals. Spread with ham mixture. Slice eggs and arrange over ham. Decorate with slices of black olive. Pour a thin layer of aspic onto a platter and allow to set. Arrange turkey over aspic and hold in place with a layer of aspic over all. Chill until firm. Trim aspic closely around each slice of turkey and remove to a lettuce-garnished platter. *6 servings.*

MOLDED SALADS

Molded Artichoke Salad

1 package frozen artichoke hearts
½ cup tomato juice
1 envelope (1 tablespoon) unflavored gelatin
1 tablespoon water
1 tablespoon lemon juice
½ cup French Dressing, page 44
1 teaspoon salt
Freshly ground pepper, to taste
½ cup mayonnaise
½ cup heavy cream, whipped
3 hard-cooked eggs, chopped
¼ cup chopped parsley
Stuffed olives, sliced
Lettuce

Cook artichokes according to package instructions until fairly well done. Drain and mash with a fork, then add tomato juice; or pour tomato juice into a blender, add artichokes and purée. Sprinkle gelatin on the mixed water and lemon juice to soften, then melt over hot water. Add to artichokes and tomato juice. Add French dressing, salt and pepper and mayonnaise. Fold in the whipped cream, chopped eggs and parsley. Rinse a 1½-quart mold in cold water, then chill it. Arrange sliced olives in a pattern on the bottom and sides of the mold. Spoon filling carefully in and chill until firm. Unmold on lettuce. 6 *servings*.

Cucumber Jelly

5 large cucumbers
1 medium onion

Peel and cube 4 of the cucumbers. Cut onion in eighths. Place in a ket-

1 quart Chicken
Broth, page 99
4 peppercorns
1 teaspoon salt
2 envelopes (2 table-
spoons) gelatin
1 cup water
2 hard-cooked eggs,
sliced
Lettuce

tle with broth, peppercorns and salt. Bring to a boil and simmer 1 hour. Strain through cheesecloth. Soften gelatin in 1 cup water and dissolve in broth. Pour into a rinsed 1½ quart mold. Refrigerate until slightly thickened. Fold in egg slices. Chill until firm. Unmold on lettuce leaves and surround with remaining cucumber, thinly sliced and fluted. *8 to 10 servings.*

Cottage-Cheese Mold

1 package (1 table-
spoon) unflav-
ored gelatin
¼ cup pineapple
juice
2½ cups creamed
cottage cheese
1 teaspoon salt
Freshly ground
pepper
½ cup chopped
parsley
½ cup pineapple
chunks
½ cup fresh straw-
berries, sliced
Lettuce

Sprinkle gelatin over pineapple juice, then dissolve over hot water. Pour into blender and add cottage cheese. Purée until very smooth. Turn into a bowl and add salt and pepper. Fold in parsley and fruits. Turn into a rinsed 1½-quart ring mold and chill until firm. Unmold on lettuce. *8 servings.*

Pitcha or Sulze (Calf's-Foot Jelly)

This should be served as an appetizer. It would be a good addition to a smörgåsbord.

2 calf's feet
2 quarts boiling water
1 teaspoon salt
1 onion
1 clove garlic
1 bay leaf
Juice of 1 lemon
2 tablespoons white vinegar
2 hard-cooked eggs

Clean calf's feet thoroughly. Soak 1 hour in cold water. Drain. Place in a heavy-bottomed pot and cover with boiling water. Add salt. Simmer 2 hours. Add onion, garlic, bay leaf, lemon juice and vinegar. Cook 1 more hour, or until very tender.

Remove meat from bones and cut into small pieces. Strain liquid through 2 thicknesses of cheesecloth wrung out in cold water. Place meat in a rinsed 1½-quart mold. Pour broth over meat. Add sliced eggs and chill until firm. Unmold. *10 to 12 servings.*

Australian Fish Mold

The recipe for this fine fish mold, which resembles the Jewish gefüllte fish, was given to me by an Australian friend who is a world traveler. Serve it as an appetizer.

3 pounds of fish heads and bones (ask your fish man for this)
1 carrot
1 onion
5 peppercorns

Make a stock by placing the fish trimmings, carrot, onion, peppercorns, celery leaves, bay leaf and salt in a large kettle and covering with water. Bring to a boil and simmer 45 minutes. Cool and strain. There should be 3½ cups liquid. Mix the finely

Celery leaves from
2 stalks
1 bay leaf
1 tablespoon salt
2 pounds ground fish
(1 pound whitefish,
½ pound carp and
½ pound yellow
pike)
4 slices white bread,
soaked in water and
squeezed dry
1 large onion, minced
Salt and pepper, to
taste
2 tablespoons ground
almonds
1 small carrot, grated
1 tablespoon
chopped parsley
2 eggs, beaten
Strips of pimiento

ground fish, bread, onion, salt and pepper, almonds, carrot, parsley and eggs together very well, then add 1½ cups of the fish stock.

Preheat oven to 300° F. Oil a 1½-quart fish-shaped mold and press the fish mixture into it firmly. Cover with aluminum foil, set in a shallow pan of hot water and bake in a 300° oven for 1½ hours, or until done; test by sticking a knife into the center. If done, the knife blade should come out clean. Cool the mold, then chill. Unmold onto a platter and decorate with strips of pimiento. Serve with sauce. *12 to 15 servings.*

Sauce:

2 eggs, beaten
Juice of 2 lemons
1 tablespoon sugar
Pinch of powdered
ginger
Salt and pepper, to
taste
2 cups boiling fish
stock (*recipe
above*)

Beat eggs with lemon juice, sugar and seasonings in top of a double boiler off the heat. Add boiling liquid very slowly, a tablespoon at a time, beating constantly. Gradually increase additions of boiling liquid until all is incorporated. Set boiler top over boiling water and cook, stirring, until of custardy consistency—mixture will coat a spoon. Cool.

Low-Calorie Cottage-Cheese Mold

1 envelope (1 tablespoon) unflavored gelatin
2 tablespoons vinegar
½ cup Chicken Broth, page 99
2 cups cottage cheese
1 teaspoon salt
Freshly ground pepper, to taste
2 teaspoons Dijon mustard
4 saccharin tablets
1 cucumber
½ cup chopped parsley
Lettuce

Sprinkle gelatin over vinegar, let soften, then melt over hot water. Place bouillon, cottage cheese, salt, pepper and mustard in blender and purée. Drop saccharin tablets in the hot vinegar and gelatin mixture. Stir until dissolved. Add to cottage-cheese mixture. Peel and chop cucumber and add. Add parsley. Rinse a 1-quart ring mold with cold water, chill it, then fill with cottage-cheese mixture. Chill until firm. Unmold on a bed of lettuce. 6 *servings.*

Head Cheese

A delicious appetizer.

1 calf's *or* pig's head
2 quarts water
2 cups white wine
1 onion
2 or 3 stalks celery
Parsley sprigs
1 carrot
1 bay leaf
5 or 6 peppercorns
1 tablespoon salt
Freshly ground
pepper, to taste
¼ teaspoon nutmeg
¼ teaspoon pow-
dered sage

Have butcher split and clean the head, setting the brains and tongue aside. Wash head thoroughly and place in a large heavy-bottomed kettle. Pour water and wine over all, using more water if needed to cover meat. Add the tongue and all remaining ingredients except pepper, nutmeg and sage. Bring to a boil and simmer 1½ hours. Remove tongue and reserve. Continue cooking head another 2½ hours.

Skin tongue and chop meat. Remove head from broth and drop well cleaned, washed brains into boiling broth. Cook 15 minutes. Remove brains and cut into small dice. Remove meat from head and dice. Strain broth through 2 layers of damp cheesecloth. Toss the meats with the pepper, nutmeg and sage. Press into an oiled 1½-quart mold. Pour in enough broth to bind the meat. Chill until set. Unmold and slice. *8 to 10 servings.*

Galantine of Chicken

1 4- to 5-pound
roasting chicken
½ pound pork, in
one piece
½ pound veal, in one
piece
¼ pound cooked
ham, in one chunk
¼ pound Italian
salami, in one
piece
1 pound fresh pork
fat
½ cup Cognac
1 tablespoon salt
1 onion, finely
chopped
Pinch of dried
thyme
1 bay leaf, crumbled
Several sprigs
parsley, finely
chopped
2 eggs, lightly
beaten
7 to 8 cups
Chicken Broth,
page 99
Choice of garnish,
as suggested below

Split chicken down the back, cut off wing tips, then remove all bones, leaving the skin intact. Be careful not to pierce skin; if it is cut, sew it up with fine cotton. (The skin becomes a case to hold the stuffing.) If you cannot face boning the chicken yourself, have your butcher do it, emphasizing that the skin must remain intact. Lay boned chicken, flesh side down, on a table and carefully loosen skin and lift from meat, taking great care when reaching the breastbone not to rip skin. Use the bones to make broth.

Cut half the pork and veal into strips about ½ inch thick and as long as you can manage. Do the same with the breast of the chicken and all of the ham and the salami. From the pork fat cut 9 strips of the same size as the other meat strips. Place all meats in a glass or plastic bowl and pour the Cognac over them. Season with ½ tablespoon of salt, onion, thyme, crumbled bay leaf and the parsley. Cover and marinate at least 2 hours or, preferably, overnight. (If to be marinated overnight, place in refrigerator.)

Make a forcemeat by grinding together very finely the remaining pork, veal and chicken. Add remaining ½ tablespoon salt, 2 eggs, beaten lightly, and the marinade drained from the meat strips.

Lay a piece of cheesecloth on a board. Slice very thin sheets of pork fat and place on the cheesecloth. Lay the chicken skin on the pork fat with flesh side up. Place a quarter of the forcemeat on the skin and pat into an oblong, leaving enough skin to overlap the finished roll. Lay alternating strips of meats and pork fat on the forcemeat. Spread another quarter of the forcemeat over strips. Repeat this pattern twice, ending with a final layer of forcemeat. Roll the stuffing up in the chicken skin, securing as tightly as possible. Skewer the skin into place, or sew roll securely. Tie the cheesecloth tightly, being sure to keep pork fat in place around the galantine.

Bring chicken broth to a boil in a deep pot with a rack. Place galantine in the boiling stock, which should only partially submerge the roll. Cover and simmer 1½ hours. Remove from broth and place on a dish. Do not remove cheesecloth. Put a plate on top of the roll and weight with several fairly heavy cans of food or other weights. Allow to cool while weighted; this makes the galantine easy to slice.

Strain the broth, which will have reduced considerably, through 2 layers of clean, damp cheesecloth. When the galantine is cool remove the cheesecloth and the sheets of pork fat and place the roll in the refrigerator. When roll is thoroughly cold, spoon a layer of the aspic formed by the broth over the meat; return to refrigerator. Decorate top of the galantine with sliced truffles, sliced stuffed olives, carrot flowers or whatever else you choose, holding garnish in place with another layer of aspic. Repeat coating and chilling process until galantine has as much aspic coating as desired.

To serve, place on a platter and surround with remaining jelled aspic, cut into small cubes; or slice the galantine and serve on a platter with garnishes of your choice. *8 to 10 servings.*

Molded Chicken Salad

3¾ cups Chicken
Broth, page 99
3 cups diced,
cooked chicken
2 envelopes (2
tablespoons) gel-
atin
¼ cup water
1 cup finely diced
celery
2 hard-cooked
eggs, chopped
½ cup mayonnaise
¼ cup chopped
scallions, green
tops and all
2 tablespoons
lemon juice
2 tablespoons
chopped pi-
miento
½ teaspoon salt
Freshly ground
pepper, to taste
Lettuce

Make chicken broth from a large fowl, as directed on page 99. Strain the broth and chill, removing all traces of fat. Remove chicken meat from the bones and dice; you should have approximately 3 cups.

Heat 3¾ cups of broth. Soften gelatin in ¼ cup cold water; dissolve in hot broth. Cool. Add the remaining ingredients and mix well. Pour into a rinsed 1½-quart mold. Chill until firm. Unmold on a platter and garnish with lettuce. *8 to 10 servings.*

MOLDED FRUIT
SALADS

Cranberry-Lemon Mold

Serve with chicken or turkey salad, or with hot poultry dishes.

2 cups cranberries, picked over
1½ cups cold water
1 cup sugar
1 envelope (1 tablespoon) un-flavored gelatin
¼ cup water
¾ cup diced celery
1 lemon, sliced paper-thin
Romaine lettuce

Wash cranberries, put into saucepan and add cold water. Cook until cranberries pop. Soften gelatin in ¼ cup water. Add sugar and gelatin to cranberries, stirring until dissolved. Chill until mixture begins to thicken, then stir in celery. Rinse a 1-quart ring mold with cold water, chill it, then arrange the paper-thin slices of lemon in the bottom. Pour cranberry mixture carefully over lemon slices. Chill until firm. Unmold onto lettuce. *8 to 10 servings.*

Fruit Mold

1 small can (15¾ ounces) pineapple chunks
1 can (11 ounces) mandarin orange sections
1 package lime gel-atin dessert
2 fresh peaches,

Drain pineapple chunks and mandarin oranges, reserving syrups. Make gelatin dessert according to package instructions, using reserved fruit juices as part of the liquid. Chill until gelatin is of egg-white consistency. Fold in the diced fruits, cherries and grapes. Rinse a 1-quart ring mold. Pour in gelatin; chill. When firm, unmold

peeled and diced
8 maraschino cher-
ries, halved
½ cup seedless
grapes
1 head chicory,
washed and
crisped
Fruit Salad Dress-
ing, page 60

onto a bed of chicory and serve with dressing. *8 servings.*

Cider Fruit Mold

Serve with a cold buffet, or in place of a salad with pork or duck.

1 envelope (1 table-
spoon) unflavored
gelatin
¼ cup cold water
3 cups apple cider
3 cloves
1 stick cinnamon
1 sprig fresh mint,
chopped
2 apples, peeled
and sliced thin
2 oranges, peeled,
sliced thin and
seeded
1 head Boston let-
tuce, washed and
crisped

Soften gelatin in cold water. Heat ci-der with cloves and cinnamon; sim-mer 15 minutes. Strain. Add gelatin and stir well. Add chopped mint. Cool.

Arrange apple and orange slices in a 1½-quart mold that has been rinsed with cold water. Pour in gelatin mix-ture. Chill until set. Unmold on a bed of Boston lettuce. *6 to 8 servings.*

CHAPTER 8

Around the World
in a Salad Bowl

M**ost**
nations have their
salad favorites,
& I am giving recipes
for only a few
of these which I hope
appeal to your palate
as much as
they do to mine.

The definition
of salad varies
among nations—
I imagine this is due
to the farming traditions
of the people.
Climate, too, has
a great influence on
salad ingredients.
The peoples of
southern lands use
marvelous
tropical fruits
in their salad dishes, while the Scandinavians use preserved
fishes and meats in conjunction with many cooked vegetables.
Far Eastern dishes are as exotic as the nations they come from.

The following recipes are typical of the regions and nations
from which they come.

UNITED STATES

Caesar Salad (California)

2 cloves garlic
1 cup olive oil
2 cans (2 ounces each) anchovy fillets
2 heads romaine, washed and crisped
1 egg
2 tablespoons lemon juice
⅓ cup good wine vinegar
1 tablespoon Worcestershire sauce
½ cup grated Parmesan cheese
2 cups toasted, unseasoned croutons
Salt, to taste
Freshly ground pepper, to taste

Crush garlic into olive oil. Add cut-up anchovy fillets and their oil. Break crisped, well-dried romaine into bite-size pieces. Place romaine in a large wooden salad bowl. Push greens aside and break raw egg into bottom. Beat egg with salad servers and toss until each leaf is well coated with egg. Add oil, anchovies, lemon juice, vinegar, Worcestershire sauce, grated Parmesan cheese and croutons. Toss well after each addition. Add salt and pepper to taste. Serve immediately. *6 to 8 servings.*

ASIA

Duck Salad

1 roasted 6-pound duck
½ cup Basic French Dressing, page 44
3 oranges
1 can (12 ounces) mandarin oranges
1 Spanish onion
1 head romaine *or* iceberg lettuce, washed and crisped
1 bunch watercress, washed and crisped
1 teaspoon grated orange peel
½ cup mayonnaise

Remove meat from duck and cube. Marinate in ¼ cup French dressing for at least 2 hours.

Remove skin and membrane from oranges and slice very thin. Remove seeds, if any. Drain mandarin oranges. Slice Spanish onion thin. Place oranges and onion in a glass bowl and pour remaining French dressing over them. Marinate for 2 hours.

Shred lettuce. Remove coarse stems from watercress. Toss with lettuce, reserving a few sprigs for garnish. Line a wooden salad bowl with the greens. Arrange duck in center of greens. Mix orange peel with mayonnaise. Mask duck with orange mayonnaise and surround with well-drained oranges and onions. Top with watercress sprigs. 6 *servings.*

BALKANS

Cucumber Salad

2 cucumbers
2 cloves garlic,
  crushed
¼ cup grated al-
  monds
¼ cup olive oil
1 tablespoon wine
  vinegar
½ teaspoon salt
  Freshly ground
  pepper, to taste
  Lettuce
  Chopped fresh
  mint, if available

Peel and chop cucumbers. Add crushed garlic, nuts, olive oil, vinegar, salt and pepper. Mix well and chill. Serve on lettuce leaves and sprinkle with mint. *6 servings.*

BELGIUM

Hot Green-Bean and Potato Salad

4 medium potatoes
1 pound fresh green beans
3 tablespoons butter
1 cup beef bouillon
6 slices bacon
⅓ cup bacon drippings
1 small onion, minced
Pinch of dried basil
Freshly ground pepper, to taste
1 teaspoon salt
4 tablespoons wine vinegar
1 cup chopped cooked ham
2 tablespoons chopped chives

Peel potatoes and slice in very fine julienne strips. Trim ends from green beans and cut each in half crosswise. Slice each piece in four lengthwise to obtain very fine strips.

Melt butter in a skillet and add potatoes, beans and bouillon. Simmer, covered, until vegetables are just done and all bouillon has been absorbed (approximately 15 minutes). Turn vegetables frequently to ensure even cooking. Cook bacon until crisp and drain fat, reserving ⅓ cup for dressing. Heat the fat and sauté onion 5 minutes without browning it. Add basil, pepper, salt and vinegar. Pour over vegetables and toss lightly. Crumble bacon over top, surround with ham and sprinkle with chives. Serve hot. *6 servings.*

CHINA

Crab Meat and Cucumber Salad

2 cans (8 ounces each) crab meat, *or* 1 pound fresh crab meat

2 cucumbers, peeled, seeded and finely chopped

2 tablespoons soy sauce

1 tablespoon vinegar

1 tablespoon sesame *or* salad oil

1 teaspoon sugar

¼ teaspoon powdered ginger

Pick the crab meat over very well, removing all traces of sinew or cartilage. Add the chopped cucumber, soy sauce, vinegar, oil, sugar and ginger. Toss lightly. Chill thoroughly. *8 servings.*

DENMARK

Curry Salad

½ cup mayonnaise
1 teaspoon curry powder, or to taste
Salt
Freshly ground pepper, to taste
Lemon juice
½ onion, grated
1 tablespoon tomato ketchup
2 cups boiled macaroni, drained and cooled
1 head romaine lettuce, washed and crisped
1 cup celery, cut into julienne strips
2 cups cooked tongue, cut into julienne strips
2 fillets marinated herring, cubed
2 hard-cooked eggs, quartered
½ bunch watercress, washed and crisped

Mix mayonnaise with curry powder, salt, pepper, lemon juice, grated onion and tomato ketchup. Toss with macaroni. Line a platter with romaine and mound macaroni in center. Arrange alternate clusters of celery and tongue strips, herring and egg quarters around macaroni. Garnish with watercress. 8 *servings.*

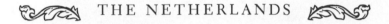 THE NETHERLANDS

Herring Salad

1 head Bibb or Boston lettuce	Wash and crisp the lettuce and line a platter with the leaves. Mix together herring, apples, eggs, boiled beets, potatoes, dill pickles and minced onion in a large bowl. Mix separately oil, vinegar, salt and pepper. Carefully bind the salad mixture with this dressing. Turn out on the platter and arrange in a mound. Mask the top and sides with mayonnaise. Surround with the pickled beets and sprinkle with chopped parsley. Chill and serve. *8 servings.*

1 head Bibb or
Boston lettuce
1 jar (8 ounces)
pickled herring in
wine sauce
3 apples, peeled and
chopped
3 hard-cooked eggs,
chopped
1 jar (1 pound)
boiled beets, well
drained and
chopped
8 cold cooked
potatoes, riced
3 dill pickles,
chopped
1 onion, minced
½ cup olive oil
3 tablespoons vine-
gar
1 teaspoon salt
¼ teaspoon freshly
ground pepper
½ cup mayonnaise
1 recipe Pickled
Beets, page 121,
drained
½ cup chopped
parsley

Wash and crisp the lettuce and line a platter with the leaves. Mix together herring, apples, eggs, boiled beets, potatoes, dill pickles and minced onion in a large bowl. Mix separately oil, vinegar, salt and pepper. Carefully bind the salad mixture with this dressing. Turn out on the platter and arrange in a mound. Mask the top and sides with mayonnaise. Surround with the pickled beets and sprinkle with chopped parsley. Chill and serve. *8 servings.*

꧁⫘ FRANCE ⫘꧂

Lobster Salad

3 cups cooked lobster meat
½ pound fresh raw button mushrooms
½ cup mayonnaise
1 teaspoon prepared mustard
Juice of ½ lemon
1 tablespoon chopped chives
¼ teaspoon celery salt
½ cup diced celery
Salt
Freshly ground pepper
Boston *or* Bibb lettuce, washed and crisped
2 whole truffles, sliced thin
Parsley sprigs

If you use fresh lobster, steam 4 small ones. Reserve shells of the claws for garnish after carefully removing the claw meat. Remove, dice and reserve all lobster body and tail meat.

Cut button mushrooms in quarters. Mix mayonnaise, mustard, lemon juice, chives and celery salt. Add mushrooms and diced celery to lobster meat and toss with mayonnaise. Add salt and pepper to taste. Line 4 large scallop shells or 4 chef-size individual salad bowls with Boston or Bibb leaves. Pile lobster on the lettuce. Garnish with truffles, a sprig of parsley and the reserved claw shells. *4 servings.*

Salade Verte Mystère

1 head romaine lettuce, washed and crisped

Break greens into bite-size pieces. Prepare cucumber by peeling strips of skin off lengthwise, leaving alternating

ᖰᖰᖰᖰᖰᖰ   FRANCE   ᖰᖰᖰᖰᖰᖰ

1 head escarole,
   washed and crisped
1 cucumber
2 small Belgian
   endives
1 cup raw mush-
   rooms, sliced
1 green pepper,
   seeded and cut
   into rings
1 recipe Mystère
   Dressing, page 49

bands. Score peeled strips with a fork. Slice paper-thin. Wash endives, drain and slice lengthwise into narrow strips. Place greens, cucumber, endives, mushrooms and pepper rings in a large wooden salad bowl. Toss with dressing. *8 servings.*

Salade Rachel

½ pound mush-
   rooms
6 cooked artichoke
   hearts, page 116
½ pound asparagus
¾ cup olive oil
¼ cup wine vinegar
3 tablespoons
   brandy
3 tablespoons port
   or sherry
   Salt and freshly
   ground pepper, to
   taste
   Chopped parsley

Drop mushrooms into boiling water and simmer 2 to 3 minutes. Cool and slice. Slice artichoke hearts. Remove heads from asparagus and place in a saucepan. Chop remaining asparagus and add to heads. Cook until barely tender. Drain well. Place all three vegetables in separate glass or ceramic bowls. Mix oil, vinegar, brandy and port or sherry together. Pour ⅓ of this mixture over each vegetable. Add salt and pepper to each bowl and marinate 2 to 3 hours. Arrange vegetables in separate mounds in a salad bowl and garnish with asparagus heads. *6 servings.*

GERMANY

Hot Potato Salad

6 medium potatoes	Wash and cook potatoes with skins
6 slices bacon	on until tender; do not overcook. Fry
¼ cup bacon drippings	bacon until crisp, drain and reserve ¼ cup of the fat. Return the ¼ cup
1½ tablespoons flour	fat to the skillet. Add the flour and
1 cup boiling water	cook over moderate heat, stirring, for
⅓ cup vinegar	2 to 3 minutes. Off heat add the boil-
1¾ teaspoons salt	ing water all at once, beating vigor-
⅛ teaspoon pepper	ously. Return to heat and cook, stir-
1 tablespoon sugar	ring, until thickened. Add vinegar,
2 stalks celery	salt, pepper and sugar and stir well.
1 cucumber, pared and scored	Remove from heat.

6 medium potatoes
6 slices bacon
¼ cup bacon drippings
1½ tablespoons flour
1 cup boiling water
⅓ cup vinegar
1¾ teaspoons salt
⅛ teaspoon pepper
1 tablespoon sugar
2 stalks celery
1 cucumber, pared and scored
2 small onions, peeled
6 red radishes, sliced
1 small head romaine lettuce, washed and crisped

Wash and cook potatoes with skins on until tender; do not overcook. Fry bacon until crisp, drain and reserve ¼ cup of the fat. Return the ¼ cup fat to the skillet. Add the flour and cook over moderate heat, stirring, for 2 to 3 minutes. Off heat add the boiling water all at once, beating vigorously. Return to heat and cook, stirring, until thickened. Add vinegar, salt, pepper and sugar and stir well. Remove from heat.

Slice celery, cucumber, onions and radishes. Break romaine into bite-size pieces. Peel and slice potatoes. Arrange alternating layers of vegetables (reserving radishes) in the skillet. Heat very slowly, tossing all together without breaking potatoes. Garnish with radishes and crumbled bacon. 8 *servings*.

GREAT BRITAIN

Dressed Crab in the Shell

4 cooked crabs	Remove all meat from crabs, carefully reserving the wide central part of the crab shells to use as serving dishes. Remove the under-shell completely and wash the hard upper-shell well. Dry it and set aside. Mix oil, vinegar and 1 teaspoon mustard. Add crumbs, parsley, salt and pepper to crab meat and dress with oil mixture. Chill well. Mix remaining mustard with 1 teaspoon water, add to mayonnaise and stir to blend. Heap crab mixture onto shells, mask with mayonnaise, sprinkle with paprika and serve. *4 servings.*
3 tablespoons olive oil	
2 tablespoons vinegar	
2 teaspoons dry mustard	
2 tablespoons fresh bread crumbs	
2 tablespoons chopped parsley	
Salt and freshly ground pepper, to taste	
⅓ cup mayonnaise	
Paprika	

GREECE

Tossed Salad

1 head romaine lettuce, washed and crisped
1 head Boston *or* iceberg lettuce, washed and crisped
1 head chicory, washed and crisped
1 can (2 ounces) anchovy fillets
1 jar (8 ounces) stuffed eggplant
1 jar (4 ounces) artichoke hearts marinated in oil
1 green pepper
1 cucumber, pared and scored
2 ripe tomatoes
½ pound Feta Cheese
Greek Dressing, page 56
8 ripe olives
1 jar (1 pound) pickled beets

Break lettuces into bite-size pieces. Drain anchovies, eggplant and artichoke hearts. Discard oil. Cut green pepper into strips. Slice cucumber and quarter tomatoes. Crumble cheese. Place all ingredients except the beets in a large wooden salad bowl. Toss with the dressing. Surround with the beets, well drained on paper towels, and the ripe olives. *8 servings.*

GREECE

Leek Salad

8 large leeks
  Few sprigs celery
  tops
1 teaspoon fennel
  seed
12 coriander seeds
½ teaspoon dried
  thyme
1 bay leaf
  Freshly ground
  pepper
1½ cups water
½ cup dry white
  wine
½ cup olive oil
½ teaspoon salt
¼ cup lemon juice

Trim leeks to within 2 inches of the white stem. Remove any roots but leave flat base of stem. Cut each leek in quarters lengthwise and wash very well. Place in a kettle.

Place celery tops, fennel, coriander, thyme and bay leaf in a square of cheesecloth and tie securely to make a *bouquet garni*. Put with all remaining ingredients in a saucepan and bring to a boil. Pour over leeks and cook over moderate heat until just tender. Discard *bouquet garni* and chill leeks in marinade. Drain before serving. 8 *servings as an hors d'oeuvre*.

HUNGARY

Corned Beef and Potato Salad

2 pounds potatoes
½ cup heavy cream
2 teaspoons pre-
  pared mustard
2 tablespoons wine
  vinegar
1 clove garlic
1 tablespoon olive
  oil
¼ cup mayonnaise
1 pound cooked
  corned beef
  Salt
  Freshly ground
  pepper
1½ pounds fresh
  sauerkraut
1 onion
2 teaspoons cara-
  way seed
1½ cups dairy sour
  cream
3 tablespoons
  water
  Paprika

Cook unpeeled potatoes until barely done. Remove skins; cut into ¼-inch slices. Make a dressing of the cream, mustard, vinegar, garlic, oil and mayonnaise. Beat until well blended. Cut corned beef into ¾-inch cubes and add to potatoes. Toss with salt and pepper to taste. Add the dressing. Press into an oiled 1½-quart mold and refrigerate.

Drain sauerkraut, taste and rinse if it is very sour. Cut onion lengthwise into thin slices; separate slices into fine strips. Place both in a bowl, add caraway seed, sour cream and water and mix well. Chill. Unmold potato salad onto a platter and surround with the sauerkraut. Garnish with a dusting of paprika. *8 to 10 servings.*

INDIA

Pachadi

This is reminiscent of Spanish Gazpacho; like that dish, it is really a soup. I would suggest serving it to precede a good hot curry.

1 cup plain yogurt
1 large tomato, peeled and finely chopped
¼ teaspoon chili powder
1 onion, minced
¼ cup chopped parsley
¼ teaspoon dry mustard
½ teaspoon ground cumin seed
½ teaspoon salt

Blend all ingredients together well and serve ice cold. *4 servings.*

ISRAEL

Eggplant Salad

1 medium eggplant
Olive oil
Juice of 1 lemon
Salt and freshly
ground pepper, to
taste
Lettuce
1 onion, finely
chopped
Tomato wedges

Heat oven to 425° and bake eggplant 30 minutes. Cool, peel completely. Mash eggplant with the back of a wooden spoon. Add oil gradually, beating constantly as you would for mayonnaise, until you reach the consistency desired. Add lemon juice, salt and pepper. Serve mounded on a lettuce leaf, sprinkled with onion and garnished with tomato wedges. *4 servings.*

ITALY

Green-Bean Salad with Tuna Dressing

¼ cup tarragon vinegar

½ teaspoon dried oregano

½ teaspoon dried basil

1 can (7 ounces) tuna fish, preferably packed in olive oil

½ cup olive oil

1 clove garlic

1 tablespoon chopped parsley

1 can (2 ounces) anchovy fillets, chopped

3 cups French-cut green beans, cooked *al dente* (still slightly crisp)

Put vinegar, oregano, basil, drained tuna fish, oil and garlic in a blender and whir until puréed. Stir in parsley and anchovies. Thin with additional oil if necessary. Pour over well-drained green beans while still hot. Cool, then chill for at least 2 hours before serving. *6 to 8 servings.*

JAPAN

Bean-Curd Salad I

Fresh and canned bean curd can be purchased in Japanese and Chinese grocery stores.

3 scallions, tops and
all, chopped
1 cucumber, peeled
and diced
2 cups bean curd
(*or* cottage
cheese), mashed
1 teaspoon salt
Freshly ground
pepper
½ cup mayonnaise

Mix all together well and serve. 6 servings.

Bean-Curd Salad II

To the above recipe add 1 tablespoon rice wine (saki) and ½ piece fresh ginger, very finely chopped.

LAOS

Chicken and Bean-Curd Salad

½ cup diced fresh
bean curd
1 tablespoon peanut
oil
1 cup cooked, diced
chicken
1 green pepper,
seeded and diced
1 cucumber, peeled
and diced
½ cup chopped fresh
mint
¼ cup coarsely
ground peanuts
½ cup minced scal-
lions
1 tablespoon peanut
oil
2 tablespoons lemon
juice
¼ cup coconut milk
obtained from a
fresh coconut
1 tablespoon sugar
Lettuce
Chopped parsley

Heat oil in a small skillet. Add bean curd and sauté until light brown in color (8 to 10 minutes). Place chicken, bean curd, green pepper and cucumber in a bowl. Mix mint, peanuts, scallions, peanut oil, lemon juice, coconut milk and sugar very well. Pour this dressing over the chicken mixture. Line a wooden bowl with lettuce and arrange chicken salad in a mound. Sprinkle with parsley. *4 servings.*

LEBANON

Caviar Salad

This salad is really an appetizer. It is to be scooped up on crackers; or cubes of bread may be dipped in it.

2 slices white bread
¼ cup lemon juice
2 cloves garlic, crushed
¼ pound caviar, red *or* black
1 cup olive oil

Trim crusts from the bread and discard them. Soak bread in water for 2 or 3 minutes; drain, then squeeze dry. Place bread, lemon juice, garlic and caviar in a blender and purée. Pour into a bowl and stir in oil. (If you do not have a blender, mash caviar and bread together, then add remaining ingredients.) *6 servings.*

MEXICO

Carne con Vinagre

4 cups very tender roast beef, cut into julienne strips
1 Spanish onion, thinly sliced
2 tablespoons chopped capers
2 tablespoons chopped parsley
1 teaspoon oregano
¾ cup Basic French Dressing, page 44

Toss meat and onion together with capers, parsley and oregano. Pour dressing over all and marinate for at least 2 hours. Chill well. *8 servings.*

NORWAY

Lamb Salad

2 cups cooked lamb, cut into julienne strips
2 cups boiled ham, cut into julienne strips
1 small onion, minced
½ cup olive oil
4 tablespoons wine vinegar
Freshly ground pepper, to taste
1 teaspoon salt
1 tablespoon chopped parsley
½ cup dairy sour cream
½ head lettuce, shredded
3 hard-cooked eggs
1 jar (1 pound) pickled beets, drained

Place lamb, ham and minced onion in a bowl and toss lightly. Put oil, vinegar, pepper, salt, parsley and sour cream in a screw-top jar and shake vigorously. Pour over meats and arrange on a bed of shredded lettuce. Garnish with wedges of hard-cooked eggs and surround with the well-drained pickled beets that have been laid on paper towels to absorb moisture. *6 servings.*

RUSSIA

Sauerkraut Salad I

*This is considered a winter salad to accompany meat or fish.
It is particularly good with roast pork.*

2 cups chilled, well-drained fresh sauerkraut
1 cup shredded carrot
½ cup olive oil
1 teaspoon salt
1 teaspoon celery seed
Lettuce cups

Taste sauerkraut and rinse if it is too sour. Mix sauerkraut and carrot well. Add oil, salt and celery seed and toss until thoroughly blended. Serve individual portions in the lettuce cups. *6 servings.*

Sauerkraut Salad II

To the above recipe add ½ cup sour cream, mixed with 2 tablespoons black caviar.

SPAIN

Ensalada

1 cup cooked lob-
   ster meat
1 can (10 ounces)
   clams, drained and
   chopped
10 to 12 small
   shrimp, cooked
1 can (10 ounces)
   white asparagus
   spears, drained
   and cut in 1-inch
   pieces
2 cups cooked,
   diced potatoes
1 cup diced celery
¼ cup thinly sliced
   onion
   White-Wine
   Mayonnaise
   (*below*)
1 head romaine let-
   tuce, washed and
   crisped
   Artichoke Hearts
   Vinaigrette, page
   117
1 can (1 pound)
   sliced beets, well
   drained
1 hard-cooked egg,
   sliced

Combine in a large bowl the lobster, clams, shrimp, asparagus, potatoes, celery and onion. Toss with ½ cup White-Wine Mayonnaise. Chill. Line a large wooden salad bowl with the romaine. Pile the salad on the lettuce and surround with the artichoke hearts, sliced beets and egg slices. Pass the remaining mayonnaise in a sauce boat. *8 servings.*

White-Wine Mayonnaise:

½ cup mayonnaise
¼ cup olive oil
3 tablespoons dry
white wine
1 teaspoon lemon
juice
1 teaspoon salt
Freshly ground
pepper, to taste
¼ teaspoon dry
mustard
1 tablespoon
chopped parsley

Combine all ingredients in a screw-top jar and shake vigorously.

 SWITZERLAND

Cheese Salad

1 head romaine lettuce, washed and crisped
6 hard-cooked eggs
½ pound Swiss cheese, shredded
¾ cup dairy sour cream
2 teaspoons Dijon mustard
1 teaspoon prepared horseradish
1 teaspoon grated lemon rind
1 teaspoon caraway seed
1 teaspoon salt
¼ teaspoon freshly ground pepper
Paprika

Chop eggs and mix with cheese. Mix sour cream, mustard, horseradish, lemon rind, caraway seed, salt and pepper to make a dressing. Mix with cheese and egg. Line a bowl with romaine. Mound salad on the lettuce and sprinkle with paprika. *6 servings.*

TURKEY

Cucumber Salad I

5 cucumbers	Peel cucumbers, cut in fourths length-
1 teaspoon salt	wise and scrape out seeds. Cut quar-
Freshly ground	ters into as many thin slices as possi-
pepper	ble. Put into a glass, plastic or ceramic
1 clove garlic	bowl. Sprinkle with salt and pepper.
1 tablespoon vinegar	Crush garlic into vinegar and mix
1 cup yogurt	with yogurt and dill. Toss with cu-
1 tablespoon	cumber, then sprinkle with mint and
chopped fresh dill	serve. Chill well before serving. 8
or ¼ teaspoon	*servings.*
dried dill weed	
1 tablespoon	
Chopped fresh	
mint	

Cucumber Salad II

To the above recipe add 1 cup grated Kaskaval or Parmesan cheese and 2 tablespoons olive oil.

CHAPTER 9

The Salad as a Complete Meal

The
salad dinner is
the greatest boon
to a busy hostess
ever invented.
The preparation can
usually be done
hours ahead &
the salad may be
assembled
just before serving;
or it may be assembled
& refrigerated
early in the day.

The glamorous
appearance of
a well-arranged
salad bowl or platter
is unsurpassed,
& the varieties
of ingredients
are endless.
❦Your whole table
may be arranged
around the salad entrée.
Buffet service
is your best choice
when presenting an elaborately arranged salad meal. Acces-
sories should be carefully chosen to add to the beauty of your
table. The centerpiece should complement the salad platter,
and the linens enhance the color scheme.

Centerpieces are often a problem for many hostesses. Beautiful arrangements can be made by using the simplest materials. Florists sell frogs of many descriptions. There are two kinds
on the market; one is a spoked metal type that impales the
stem of the flower; the other is a soft spongelike material that
absorbs water—the stem of a flower forced down into this substance is quite secure and will not capsize if the vase is jarred.

Consider the season when arranging a table setting. You will
wonder what natural materials can be used in midwinter, but
take the bare branch of a dogwood tree, for instance. The Oriental appearance of this tree, especially when bare, is stunning.
You can leave untouched the natural bark color of the branch
or spray it with white paint. Force the cut end down onto the
spokes of a metal frog and stand it in a shallow wooden, ce-

ramic or glass bowl. Arrange evergreen sprigs around the frog to hide it. If your bowl is ceramic or glass, melt the ends of your candles and press down onto the bowl, securing them as the wax cools.

It is not necessary to spend a fortune at the florist. The centerpiece and decorations you make yourself are infinitely more rewarding. Spring, summer and fall, of course, offer endless suggestions. Wild flowers and many weeds make beautiful bouquets if you use imagination. Leaves alone, whether evergreen or deciduous, present fine effects. Vegetables, especially during the harvest season, can make a most interesting tablepiece. If you combined both fruits and vegetables you would have a "horn o' plenty" arrangement. Utilize your house plants in a pinch. Always have fresh new candles on hand to accommodate last-minute plans. Flower-arranging intimidates many women, but you should try to see if you can achieve appealing results.

Menu suggestions accompany each recipe in this chapter.

JELLIED CONSOMMÉ MADRILÈNE,
page 100
.

*SALADE NIÇOISE
.

THINLY SLICED, BUTTERED
BLACK BREAD
.

FRESH PINEAPPLE CHILLED
IN SWEET WINE
.

COOKIES OF YOUR CHOICE
.

BEVERAGE

Salade Niçoise

A *classic French salad.*

3 cups freshly cooked and sliced potatoes

¼ cup dry white wine

3 cups French-cut green beans, cooked until barely tender (*al dente*)

1 cup Basic French Dressing, page 44

1 head Boston lettuce

2 cans (7 ounces each) Italian *or* French tuna fish (packed in olive oil)

2 cans (2 ounces each) anchovy fillets

3 hard-cooked eggs, quartered

½ cup black olives, pitted

1 tablespoon chopped chives

1 tablespoon chopped parsley

While potatoes are still warm, pour wine over them and marinate for at least 1 hour. Place the green beans in a glass or plastic bowl and pour ⅓ cup French dressing over them. Marinate at least 1 hour, preferably longer. Cut out the core of the lettuce and very carefully separate the leaves. Wash them and allow to crisp without losing their cup-like shape. Drain the tuna fish and break into bite-size pieces. Drain and separate the anchovy fillets.

Using either a large salad bowl or platter, arrange a mound of potatoes in the center. Encircle with the cups of lettuce. In the cups arrange alternately mounds of green beans, tuna, eggs, olives and anchovy fillets. Sprinkle with the chopped chives and parsley. Allow each guest to serve himself from the platter. Pass a cruet with the remaining French dressing. *8 servings.*

POTAGE SENEGALESE, *page* 102

•

*ALI-BABA SALAD

•

BUTTERED ROLLS

•

VANILLA ICE CREAM WITH CURAÇAO

•

CHOCOLATE WAFERS

•

BEVERAGE

Ali-Baba Salad

2 large sweet potatoes *or* yams
½ cup olive oil *or* other salad oil
¼ cup wine vinegar
2 tablespoons honey
½ teaspoon salt
Freshly ground pepper, to taste
¼ cup water
4 small zucchini
Basic French Dressing, page 44
2 pounds raw shrimp
4 quarts water
1 onion, quartered
1 bay leaf
1 teaspoon salt
½ cup mayonnaise
3 tablespoons prepared horseradish
2 tablespoons chopped chives
3 tablespoons chopped parsley
1 head romaine lettuce, washed and crisped
3 tomatoes, cut in wedges
3 hard-cooked eggs, quartered

Peel sweet potatoes or yams and cut into julienne strips. Place in a saucepan with the oil, wine vinegar, honey, salt, pepper and water. Cook uncovered until barely tender. Chill in the marinade. Scrub zucchini and drop whole into boiling salted water and cook until barely tender; they should be slightly crisp to the bite. Drain and cut into ¼-inch slices. Marinate in ½ cup French dressing for at least 2 hours.

Clean and devein shrimp. Drop into 4 quarts boiling water with the onion, bay leaf and salt and cook until just pink—do not overcook. Drain and chill.

Mix mayonnaise with horseradish, chives and 1 tablespoon parsley. Toss with chilled shrimp.

Shred lettuce and place in bottom of salad bowl. Toss with ⅓ cup French dressing. Arrange shrimp on lettuce. Arrange the potatoes, zucchini, tomatoes and eggs alternately around the shrimp. Sprinkle with remaining parsley. *8 servings.*

GAZPACHO, *page* 105

·

*AVOCADO, CRAB MEAT
AND POTATO SALAD

·

HOT BUTTERED ITALIAN BREAD

·

RASPBERRY BOMBE

·

ICED COFFEE

Avocado, Crab Meat and Potato Salad

2 cups fresh or
canned crab meat
½ green pepper, very
finely chopped
1 stalk celery, very
finely chopped
1 small onion,
grated
⅔ cup mayonnaise
3 tablespoons dry
sherry
Salt and pepper,
to taste
1 bunch watercress,
washed and
crisped
1 head romaine let-
tuce, washed and
crisped
4 large ripe
avocados
Juice of 2 lemons
3 cups French
Potato Salad,
page 128
Paprika

Pick crab meat over well, removing all bits of cartilage and shell. Mix with green pepper, celery, onion, mayonnaise, sherry, salt and pepper. Set aside. Separate watercress into attractive bunches. Separate romaine leaves and set aside the most attractive ones. Just before serving, peel the avocados and halve, being careful to keep each half intact. Brush avocado halves with lemon juice to prevent discoloration.

Arrange romaine leaves on a platter and mound the potato salad in the center. Pile the crab mixture in the avocado cups and place around potatoes. Garnish generously with the watercress and sprinkle potato salad with paprika. *8 servings.*

VICHYSSOISE, *page 104*

·

*SALADE BRESSANE

·

SLICED TOMATOES
IN FRENCH DRESSING

·

HOME-MADE WHITE BREAD

·

STRAWBERRY TART

·

BEVERAGE

Salade Bressane

2 cups asparagus tips, cooked

1 green pepper, seeded and cut into thin rings

¾ cup Basic French Dressing, page 44

2 heads lettuce of your choice, washed and crisped

16 slices cooked breast of chicken

3 tablespoons olive oil

1 tablespoon lemon juice

Salt and pepper, to taste

2 tablespoons chopped parsley

1 cup mayonnaise

½ teaspoon paprika

1 tablespoon tomato paste

4 hard-cooked eggs, quartered

3 truffles, thinly sliced

Marinate asparagus and green-pepper rings for at least 1 hour in ½ cup French dressing. Shred lettuce and place in a large wooden salad bowl or on a platter. Toss with ¼ cup French dressing. Season chicken slices with oil, lemon juice, salt, pepper and parsley. Place slices symmetrically over shredded lettuce. Mix mayonnaise with paprika and tomato paste. Mask the chicken slices with a thin coating of the mayonnaise. Between chicken slices place the asparagus tips. Garnish the whole with pepper rings and quartered hard-cooked eggs. Arrange a slice or two of truffle on each chicken slice. 8 *servings*.

UKRAINIAN BORSCHT, *page 106*

·

*MAHARAJAH SALAD

·

ANNE'S GREEK CUCUMBER SALAD, *page 125*

·

SACHER TORTE

·

BEVERAGE

Maharajah Salad

1 teaspoon curry powder, or to taste
1 cup Basic French Dressing, page 44
2 cups cooked crab meat
3 cups cooked rice
3 small zucchini
4 stalks celery
4 tomatoes
Salt, to taste
Freshly ground pepper, to taste
4 hard-cooked eggs
¼ cup chopped chives
1 quart shredded lettuce
1 head Boston lettuce, washed and crisped

Blend curry powder into ½ cup French dressing. Pick over crab meat to remove all cartilage or bits of shell. Toss with rice. Pour curried dressing over rice and crab meat and place in refrigerator for several hours. Scrub zucchini and cook in boiling salted water until barely tender. Cut into ¼-inch slices. Pour remaining French dressing over zucchini and marinate at least 1 hour. Chill.

Cut celery into julienne strips. Quarter tomatoes, remove any watery pulp and sprinkle with salt and pepper. Remove yolks from eggs and set aside for other uses. Chop the whites very fine and add to the chopped chives.

Place shredded lettuce in salad bowl. Arrange several large leaves of Boston lettuce in center of bowl. Mound rice and crab mixture on these leaves. Place remaining leaves of Boston lettuce around edges of bowl. Drain zucchini and reserve dressing. Arrange alternating spoonsful of zucchini, celery and tomatoes around the rice and crab mixture and over the Boston lettuce. Sprinkle the whole with the chopped egg whites and chives. Pour French dressing (use that in which zucchini was marinated) over the whole just before serving. *8 servings.*

COLD STRAWBERRY SOUP, *page 111*

·

*SALADE À L'ALLEMANDE

·

HOT GARLIC BREAD

·

PEARS WITH RASPBERRY SAUCE

·

COOKIES OF YOUR CHOICE

ICED TEA

Salade à l'Allemande

3 medium-size, freshly boiled potatoes
1 tart eating apple
4 tablespoons mayonnaise
1 head Boston lettuce, washed and crisped
1 Spanish onion
1 jar (1 pound) sliced pickled beets
2 or 3 fillets of pickled herring, sliced in ½-inch pieces
2 cups tongue, cut into julienne strips
1 large dill pickle, cut into julienne strips
Chopped parsley
½ cup Basic French Dressing, page 44

Dice the potatoes and the apple and toss with the mayonnaise. Line a large wooden salad bowl or a platter with cups of lettuce and mound the potato mixture in the middle. Thinly slice the onion and arrange slices fanwise around the potatoes, alternating with the very well drained beets. Arrange the herring, tongue and pickles attractively around the potatoes, onions and beets. Sprinkle parsley over all. Just before serving pour the dressing over the whole. *8 servings.*

COLD CUCUMBER SOUP, *page* 102

·

*CHICKEN SALAD ORIENTALE

·

ARTICHOKE HEARTS VINAIGRETTE,
page 117

·

CHILLED RICE PUDDING
WITH SLICED STRAWBERRIES
AND WHIPPED CREAM

·

ICED TEA WITH LEMON

Chicken Salad Orientale

3 tablespoons olive
oil
2 tablespoons soy
sauce
1 tablespoon cider
vinegar
2 teaspoons sugar
¼ teaspoon
powdered ginger
⅛ teaspoon
cinnamon
1 clove garlic,
minced
1 small onion
2 hard-cooked eggs
3 cups diced
cooked chicken
3 cups Chinese cab-
bage, cut into ¼-
inch strips
1 cup celery, cut
into ¼-inch diag-
onal strips
1 can (1 pound)
sliced bamboo
shoots, well
drained and
chilled
1 head romaine let-
tuce, washed and
crisped

Put oil, soy sauce, vinegar, sugar, ginger, cinnamon and garlic in the
blender and whirl for a few seconds.
(If you do not have a blender, beat
very well together until thoroughly
blended.) Chill well. Cut onion
lengthwise into very thin slices; separate into very thin strips. Chop eggs.
Toss chicken, Chinese cabbage, celery, bamboo shoots and onion with
dressing. Arrange lettuce on a platter
or in a wooden salad bowl. Mound
the chicken mixture on lettuce and
sprinkle with chopped egg. 8 *servings*.

ANTIPASTO, *page 77*

•

*ELEGANT CHICKEN SALAD PLATE

•

BEAN SALAD, *page 119*

•

STRAWBERRY SHORTCAKE

•

COFFEE

Elegant Chicken Salad Plate

3 cups cooked
  chicken, diced
½ cup finely
  chopped celery
½ cup finely
  chopped green
  pepper
3 large cucumbers
1 cup dry white
  wine
¾ cup mayonnaise
1 teaspoon curry
  powder, or to taste
1 teaspoon chopped
  chives
1 teaspoon chopped
  parsley
  Lettuce of your
  choice, washed
  and crisped
1 Spanish onion,
  sliced in rings
2 cups Green-Bean
  Salad Vinaigrette,
  page 118
8 radish flowers
3 hard-cooked eggs,
  quartered
1 teaspoon capers

Mix chicken, celery and green pepper. Peel cucumber and use a small melon scoop to cut out 12 small balls. Add to chicken mixture. Marinate in the wine for 2 to 3 hours. Mix mayonnaise with curry powder, chives and parsley. Toss with chicken mixture. Arrange lettuce leaves on a platter. Mound chicken on lettuce and surround with onions, green beans, radish flowers and egg quarters. Sprinkle with capers. 6 to 8 servings.

JELLIED CONSOMMÉ MADRILÈNE,
page 100

·

*ARTICHOKE AND TONGUE SALAD

·

PUMPERNICKEL WITH HERB BUTTER

·

CHEESE AND CRACKERS

·

FRUIT

·

COFFEE

Artichoke and Tongue Salad

3 hearts of celery
1 recipe Artichoke
  Hearts Vinai-
  grette, page 117
2 tablespoons
  tomato paste
½ cup mayonnaise
3 cups cooked and
  cooled macaroni
  Salt and pepper,
  to taste
  Iceberg lettuce
  cups, washed and
  crisped
4 hard-cooked eggs
16 slices freshly
  cooked tongue
  Black olives
  Chopped parsley

Cut celery hearts into julienne strips. Prepare Artichoke Hearts Vinaigrette and cool. Cut each heart into bite-size pieces. Stir tomato paste into mayonnaise and toss with celery, artichoke hearts and macaroni. Season to taste with salt and pepper. Mound in lettuce cups in a salad bowl or on a platter. Arrange slices of egg and tongue around the salad. Garnish with olives and a sprinkling of parsley. *8 servings.*

CREAM OF PEA SOUP WITH MINT,
page 101

·

*MACÉDOINE OF VEGETABLES
WITH TURKEY SLICES IN ASPIC*

·

HOT BUTTERED SCONES

·

BAKED ALASKA

·

DEMITASSE

Macédoine of Vegetables
with Turkey Slices in Aspic

1 cup diced carrots, cooked and drained

1 cup French-cut green beans, cooked and drained

1 medium onion, finely chopped

1 cup peas, cooked and drained

1 cup asparagus tips, cooked and drained

1 recipe English Mayonnaise, page 48

2 recipes Quick Aspic made with chicken broth, page 139

16 slices turkey breast ¼ inch thick

2 truffles, sliced thin, or 16 stuffed olives, sliced

1 head Boston lettuce, washed and crisped

4 tomatoes, cut into wedges

Chopped parsley

Mix the first five vegetables with mayonnaise and allow to marinate for several hours in the refrigerator. Pour a thin layer of aspic on a large platter, then place the turkey slices on top. Pour another thin layer of aspic over all and allow to set. Put a slice of truffle or several slices of olive on top of each slice. Very carefully pour another layer of aspic over the slices to secure the garnish. Allow to set. Pour a final coat over all. When aspic has set finally, cut each slice out carefully, following the contours of the turkey. Arrange lettuce leaves in a ring on a large platter. Pile the macédoine of vegetables in the center. Carefully lift turkey aspics with a spatula and place on the lettuce leaves. Decorate with wedges of tomato. Sprinkle turkey aspics with parsley. *8 servings.*

TOMATO-JUICE COCKTAIL

·

*CHEF'S SALAD BOWLS

·

HOT BUTTERED FRENCH BREAD

·

RICH DARK CHOCOLATE CAKE
À LA MODE

·

COFFEE

Chef's Salad

1 head Boston
lettuce, washed
and crisped
1 head romaine
lettuce, washed
and crisped
1 head chicory,
washed and
crisped
1 bunch watercress,
washed and
crisped
1 cucumber, sliced
Green-Bean Salad
with Tuna Dress-
ing, page 179
2 cups cooked ham,
cut into julienne
strips
2 cups salami, cut
into julienne
strips
1 pound Swiss
cheese, cut into
julienne strips
4 hard-cooked eggs,
quartered
24 cherry tomatoes
1 recipe Chef's
Salad Dressing,
page 56

Break lettuces and chicory into bite-size pieces. Toss with watercress and cucumber. Divide among 8 individual chef-size salad bowls. Place a mound of Green-Bean Salad in the center of each bowl. Arrange alternating bundles of ham, salami and cheese strips around beans. Garnish with eggs and cherry tomatoes. Pass Chef's Salad Dressing in a cruet. 8 *servings.*

CHAPTER 10
A Thing of Beauty,
a Joy to Behold
The Luncheon Salad

Τhe
luncheon salad
differs from
the complete-meal
salad in that
it is far less hearty
& caters more
to the delicate appetite.

One tends
to associate it with
ladies' bridge parties
& membership meetings;
however, a luncheon salad
may be made hearty enough
to please
the most robust
masculine taste.
Luncheon salads may be
made with any
number of ingredients;
fruit, cheeses, fish,
fowl or meat, all types of vegetables, herbs, spices and dressings.

Vegetable and fruit shells stuffed with fish or fowl mixtures are truly elegant. All manner of aspics and gelatin molds are suitable for luncheons. The only basic requirement is attractive arrangement. Each salad is usually arranged beautifully as an individual serving—luncheon salads are rarely served in a large bowl.

A great convenience for luncheon salads is the individual chef-size wooden bowl. Larger than the average size by perhaps three inches, this bowl allows attractive presentation of many types of salads.

Dressings for luncheon salads may be sweet or tart, depending on taste and the foods to be complemented. The best way to serve dressings is in a separate cruet or boat which is passed from guest to guest. More than one dressing may be used in order to offer a choice, or when you are presenting both fruits and vegetables.

I suggest the following luncheon menus, one to precede each recipe. Menus and recipes are suitable for card-party luncheons; however, they could be used for any important midday occasion. Always remember the importance of eye appeal, and appoint your table accordingly. I have tried to remember this eye appeal in my menu suggestions. I hope the colors harmonize and our tastes are alike!

JELLIED CONSOMMÉ MADRILÈNE,
page 100

·

*STUFFED AVOCADO SALAD PLATE

·

HOT SCONES

·

ORANGE SHERBET AND COOKIES

·

ICED COFFEE

·

Stuffed Avocado Salad Plate

3 large ripe avocados

Juice of 2 lemons

1 head chicory, washed and crisped

3 cups chopped, cooked shrimp

1 teaspoon chopped capers

3 hard-cooked eggs

3 scallions, finely chopped, green tops and all

1 teaspoon salt

Freshly ground pepper, to taste

¾ cup English Mayonnaise, page 48

6 sprigs parsley

12 whole cooked shrimp

1 green pepper, seeded and cut into rings

1 jar (1 pound) pickled beets, well drained

2 tomatoes, cut into wedges

Pitted black olives

French Dressing with herbs, page 45

Peel avocados and halve them, carefully removing the pits. Brush all over with lemon juice to prevent discoloration. Place each half on a bed of chicory on an individual salad plate. Toss chopped shrimp, capers, eggs, scallions, salt and pepper in a bowl with the mayonnaise. Heap into centers of avocado halves. Garnish each portion with a sprig of parsley and 2 whole shrimp.

Surround each avocado half with 3 or 4 green-pepper rings. Place several slices of pickled beet in the center of each ring. Intersperse wedges of tomato with the green-pepper rings. Add a few black olives. Pass herbed French dressing in a cruet. *6 servings.*

ICED RASPBERRY SOUP, *page 110*

·

*STUFFED TOMATO SALAD PLATE

·

HOT BUTTERED DINNER ROLLS

·

PISTACHIO ICE CREAM
WITH CRÈME DE CACAO

·

COFFEE OR TEA

Stuffed Tomato Salad Plate

6 large beefsteak
tomatoes
2 cans (7 ounces
each) crab meat,
or 2 cups fresh-
cooked crab meat,
well picked over
2 tablespoons
lemon juice
1 small onion,
grated
1 teaspoon salt
Freshly ground
pepper, to taste
2 tablespoons
chopped parsley
¾ cup mayonnaise
substitute with
capers, page 66
6 sprigs parsley
1 head romaine
lettuce, washed
and crisped
1 cucumber, peeled,
scored and sliced
1 recipe Artichoke
Hearts
Vinaigrette,
page 117
3 hard-cooked eggs,
quartered

Choose very large red tomatoes of uniform size. Drop into a pot of boiling water for 5 seconds, remove and slip off skins. Cut the stem end off each tomato and hollow out the center by removing seeds and pulp, leaving the shell intact. Toss together the crab meat, lemon juice, onion, salt, pepper, chopped parsley and mayonnaise. Heap into tomato shells and decorate each with a sprig of parsley.

Arrange several leaves of romaine on each of 6 plates. Place a stuffed tomato, several slices of cucumber and 2 or 3 Artichoke Hearts Vinaigrette on romaine. Garnish with wedges of egg. *6 servings.*

FRENCH ONION SOUP

·

ARTICHOKE SURPRISE

·

HOT FRENCH BREAD

·

SEVEN-LAYER CAKE

·

HOT COFFEE

Artichoke Surprise

6 large artichokes
1 teaspoon salt
2 cans (7 ounces each) crab meat or salmon
Juice of 1 lemon
½ cup mayonnaise
Salt, to taste
Freshly ground pepper, to taste
1 onion, grated
1 head Boston or Bibb lettuce, washed and crisped
Green-Bean Salad Vinaigrette, page 118
3 tomatoes, cut into wedges

Wash artichokes carefully, removing any unsightly outer leaves. Cut the tips off the large outer leaves. Stand on a rack in a deep pot and pour in approximately 2 inches of boiling water. Add salt, cover tightly and simmer 45 minutes. Drain and cool artichokes. Remove the choke by parting center leaves and carefully scooping out the fuzzy core, leaving the heart intact. Mash the crab meat or salmon and mix with lemon juice, mayonnaise, salt and pepper and onion. Place a small amount of this paste carefully in hollow of each artichoke leaf without detaching the leaf from the heart. Fill the center hollow with fish mixture.

On 6 individual plates, arrange beds of Boston or Bibb lettuce. Place a stuffed artichoke in the center of each, surround with Green-Bean Salad Vinaigrette and garnish with tomato wedges.

With each individual salad provide an empty saucer for discarded leaves. To eat, pull off a leaf containing stuffing, place in mouth and draw through teeth, enjoying the pulp of the artichoke leaf with the fish stuffing. The fish-filled artichoke center may be eaten with a knife and fork when all leaves have been consumed. *6 servings.*

CHILLED CRANBERRY JUICE

·

*INDIVIDUAL CREAM·CHEESE MOLDS

·

HOMEMADE HERB BREAD

·

STRAWBERRY TART

·

TEA OR COFFEE

Individual Cream-Cheese Molds

2 packages (6 ounces each) cream cheese
1 cup mayonnaise
½ teaspoon salt
1 onion, minced
2 tablespoons chopped parsley
¼ teaspoon garlic powder
Juice of 1 lemon
1 envelope (1 tablespoon) unflavored gelatin
¼ cup water
2 cucumbers, peeled, seeded and chopped
Stuffed olives, sliced
1 head romaine, washed and crisped
1½ pounds cooked, shelled and deveined shrimp
Horseradish Cocktail Dressing, page 57

Bring cream cheese to room temperature. Mash, then add mayonnaise, salt, onion, parsley, garlic powder and lemon juice. Soak gelatin in water, then heat over hot water until melted. Beat into cream cheese. Fold in cucumbers. Rinse 6 individual ring molds in cold water. Place olive slices in bottom and pour cream-cheese mixture carefully over them. Chill until firm. Unmold onto beds of romaine lettuce on 6 individual plates.

Surround molds with shrimp. Fill centers of molds with Horseradish Cocktail Sauce. 6 *servings*.

CHILLED TOMATO JUICE

·

*SAUERKRAUT AND HAM IN ASPIC

·

FRENCH BREAD

·

PARIS-BREST

·

DEMITASSE

Sauerkraut and Ham in Aspic

3 cups sauerkraut, canned or fresh
4 cups Chicken Broth, page 99
2 medium onions
1 envelope (1 tablespoon) unflavored gelatin
¼ cup water
½ cup olive oil
3 tablespoons vinegar
½ teaspoon salt
Freshly ground pepper, to taste
4 tablespoons sugar
1 cup diced, cooked ham
1 head Boston or Bibb lettuce, washed and crisped
3 hard-cooked eggs, quartered
1 jar (1 pound) sliced, pickled beets
Green olives

Place drained sauerkraut, broth and onions in a saucepan and cook, covered, 40 minutes. Soften gelatin in ¼ cup water and add to boiling sauerkraut. Cook 5 minutes. Remove onions, chop and return to saucepan. Cool. Add oil, vinegar, salt, pepper and sugar. Fold in ham. Divide mixture among 6 individual molds which have been previously rinsed in cold water (glass custard cups can be used). Allow to set.

When molds are firm, turn out on lettuce leaves on 6 individual salad plates. (To unmold, dip in hot water for 5 or 6 seconds. Place a wet spatula over the mold and quickly invert, releasing jelly. Slip from spatula onto the lettuce.) Surround with egg quarters and the well-drained pickled beets. Garnish with green olives. 6 *servings.*

FRUIT CUP

·

*SALMON MOUSSE

·

LEMON CHIFFON PIE

·

COFFEE OR TEA

Salmon Mousse

2 pounds fresh
  salmon
1 teaspoon salt
2 stalks celery, tops
  included
4 peppercorns
1 bay leaf
1 onion, quartered
2 cups Quick Aspic
  (page 139) made
  with fish poach-
  ing liquid
½ cup thick
  Béchamel Sauce,
  page 73
1 teaspoon salt
¼ teaspoon pepper
2 tablespoons
  chopped parsley
  Juice of 1 lemon
1 tablespoon
  chopped capers
½ cup heavy cream,
  whipped
1 head Boston
  lettuce, washed
  and crisped
2 green peppers,
  cut into rings
12 deviled egg halves
  (see page 78)
  Caviar Mayon-
  naise, page 47

Wrap the fish in 2 thicknesses of cheesecloth. Place a rack in a heavy-bottomed pot. Pour 2 inches of water into the bottom and bring to a boil. Add salt, cut-up celery, peppercorns, bay leaf and onion. Place fish on the rack and poach 20 to 30 minutes, or until fish flakes easily when pierced with a fork. Remove from broth and cool. Strain broth and use to make the Quick Aspic, adding clam juice as needed to make 2 cups of recipe.

Remove all bones and skin from the salmon and mash flesh. Add béchamel sauce, salt, pepper, parsley, lemon juice and capers; mix. Fold in whipped cream. Rinse and chill 6 individual molds. Pour a small amount of aspic into each ice-cold mold and swirl around quickly. Place in the refrigerator until very firm. Repeat this process until there is a shell of aspic approximately ¹⁄₁₆ inch thick. Firmly pack the cavity with the salmon mousse. Pour a thin coating of aspic over top. Chill again until firm.

Unmold onto beds of lettuce on individual plates and encircle with green-pepper rings and the deviled eggs. Pass a boat of caviar mayonnaise. 6 servings.

HONEYDEW WEDGES WITH LEMON

·

SALMON STEAKS IN ASPIC

·

BREAD STICKS

·

STRAWBERRY PARFAIT

·

COFFEE

Salmon Steaks in Aspic

1 onion, quartered
1 stalk celery, cut
  into 1-inch pieces
1 sprig parsley
1 carrot, cut into
  chunks
1 bay leaf
1 teaspoon salt
  Freshly ground
  pepper, to taste
6 salmon steaks
  Fish Aspic, page
  138
3 hard-cooked eggs,
  sliced
  Capers
1 head chicory,
  washed and crisped
  French Potato
  Salad, page 128
  Sliced beefsteak
  tomatoes

Place a rack in a good-size kettle that will comfortably accommodate the salmon steaks in one layer. Put the onion, celery, parsley, carrot, bay leaf, salt and pepper in the kettle and add enough water to cover rack and fish. Place fish on the rack, bring to a boil, cover and simmer 15 to 20 minutes, or until salmon flakes easily when flicked with a fork. Remove from heat and allow to cool in the poaching liquid.

Remove steaks from poaching liquid and carefully take center bones out. Remove skin, keeping steaks intact. Pour a thin layer of aspic on a platter large enough to hold the steaks. Allow aspic to set, then lay salmon on aspic. Arrange slices of egg on top and decorate carefully with a few capers. Spoon aspic over all, being careful not to dislodge decorations. Allow to set. Repeat process until salmon is sufficiently coated.

Arrange beds of chicory on 6 individual salad plates. When aspic is thoroughly set, cut around steaks and remove with a spatula to beds of lettuce. Chop excess aspic and surround salmon steaks with it. Place a spoonful of the potato salad and a few slices of tomato on each plate. 6 *servings*.

FRESH FRUIT CUP

·

*MOLDED CHEF'S SALAD PLATE

·

ROLLS

·

APPLE PIE AND CHEDDAR CHEESE

·

COFFEE OR TEA

Molded Chef's Salad Plate

1 cup cooked
  tongue, cut into
  julienne strips
1 cup cooked ham,
  cut into julienne
  strips
1 cup Swiss cheese,
  cut into julienne
  strips
1 cup cooked green
  beans, cut into
  ½-inch pieces
½ cup cooked peas
½ cup shredded raw
  carrots
1 tablespoon grated
  onion
  Salt to taste
  Freshly ground
  pepper, to taste
1 recipe Classic
  Tomato Aspic,
  page 141
1 head Boston
  lettuce, washed
  and crisped
6 hard-cooked eggs,
  quartered
  Stuffed olives
1 recipe Mayon-
  naise with herbs,
  page 47

Toss together the tongue, ham, cheese, beans, peas, carrots and onion; season with salt and pepper. Pack into 6 individual molds. Pour tomato aspic in to fill molds and chill until firm.

Line individual chef-size salad bowls or salad plates with Boston lettuce and unmold the aspics. Garnish each with wedges of egg and several olives. Pass a boat of herbed mayonnaise when serving. *6 servings.*

VICHYSSOISE, *page* 104

·

SHRIMP IN PINEAPPLE CASINGS

·

MELBA TOAST

·

HOMEMADE POUND CAKE

·

DEMITASSE

Shrimp in Pineapple Casings

3 small ripe pineapples
3 oranges
2 avocados
Fresh lemon juice
2 pounds shrimp, cooked, shelled and deveined
Dressing (*below*)

Halve the pineapples lengthwise, leaving half of the leaves with each portion. Scoop out fruit, leaving shell approximately ½ inch thick. Discard hard inner core and chop fruit. Peel oranges and remove all white membrane; cut into small pieces. Peel and slice avocado and brush all sides with lemon juice to prevent discoloration. Place fruits and the shrimp in a bowl and toss with the dressing. Heap into pineapple shells. *6 servings.*

Dressing:

¼ cup dry white wine
Juice of 2 lemons
1 tablespoon honey
1 teaspoon salt
1 cup olive oil
1 tablespoon chopped fresh mint, *or* 1 teaspoon dried mint

Place all ingredients in a screw-top jar and shake vigorously. *Makes 1½ cups.*

TOMATO   JUICE

·

*SEAFOOD-STUFFED   RICE   RING

·

SACHER   TORTE

·

COFFEE

Seafood-Stuffed Rice Ring

3 cups cold cooked
rice
¼ cup Basic French
Dressing, page 44
3 tablespoons
chopped chives
1 can (7 ounces)
tuna fish
1 pound cooked
shrimp, shelled,
deveined and
chopped
½ cup finely
chopped celery
1 cup mayonnaise
2 tablespoons
lemon juice
1 teaspoon curry
powder, or to
taste
Boston *or* iceberg
lettuce, washed
and crisped
Capers

Toss rice with French dressing and chives. Drain and flake tuna fish and place in a bowl with shrimp and celery. Mix mayonnaise, lemon juice and curry powder. Toss fish with mayonnaise and chill.

Arrange cups of lettuce on 6 salad plates. Divide rice in 6 portions and arrange in a ring on each lettuce bed. Fill the ring with tuna and shrimp mixture. Garnish with capers and serve. *6 servings.*

FRESH SHRIMP COCKTAIL

·

*STUFFED BAKED BEET
LUNCHEON PLATE

·

HOT FRENCH BREAD

·

CHILLED CARAMEL CUSTARD

·

COFFEE

Stuffed Baked Beet Luncheon Plate

8 large beets
3 hard-cooked eggs
¼ pound sliced
    cooked ham
¼ teaspoon salt
    Freshly ground
    pepper, to taste
¼ cup mayonnaise
8 sprigs parsley
1 head iceberg
    lettuce, washed
    and crisped
1 recipe Asparagus
    Spears Vinai-
    grette, page 117
1 recipe Potato
    Salad with Cham-
    pagne, page 129

Preheat oven to 375° F. Wash beets and cut stems close to base. Place in preheated oven and bake until beets give a little when pressed with a finger (approximately 1 hour). Remove from oven and cool. Slip off skins and cut each beet in half. With a spoon or sharp knife hollow out the halves, leaving a shell about ½ inch thick. Chop the scooped-out beet fine. Chop the hard-cooked eggs and the ham. Season to taste and toss with mayonnaise. Fold chopped beet in carefully, discoloring the egg and ham as little as possible. Mound the stuffing into beet cups. Garnish each with a sprig of parsley.

Arrange cups of lettuce on 8 individual salad plates. Place 2 stuffed beet halves on each plate. Surround with mounds of asparagus and potato salad. *8 servings.*

CHAPTER 11

Les Pièces de Résistance

Fruit Salads in All Their Glory

Luscious
chilled fruits
lend themselves
admirably to
the salad course.
Fruit salads
can be served as
appetizer, salad course
or dessert.

Fruits can be stuffed,
molded into
gelatin mixtures,
or tossed with
a variety of dressings.
They can be sweet,
tart or both.
They can be served
in a bowl,
on a platter or on
individual plates.
Combine fruits
with greens, nuts
or certain vegetables; combine them with fowl, fish or meat.
What more can I say about nature's most succulent gift? I
can only suggest some of the many uses of fruit. Serve the
following salads at any point in the meal that you feel would
best suit your menu.

A word on preparing citrus fruits: While in Europe I
learned a way to cut these fruits that is superior to our American way of peeling oranges and grapefruit, then cutting them
into wedges. Peel the fruit by slicing the two ends off; then
cut all skin and membrane off in lengthwise strips, from one
cut end to the other. Slice the peeled fruit ¼ inch thick. Seeds
and any unwanted parts can be removed without spoiling the
beauty of the fruit. The circles can be halved or quartered
for use in compotes and salads, if desired.

FRUIT SALADS TO
ACCOMPANY
MEAT OR POULTRY

Apple Cups

This salad is good with roast pork.

6 large, firm red apples
1 cup chopped walnuts
3 tablespoons bland oil
1 tablespoon lemon juice
½ teaspoon sugar
1 cup diced celery
½ cup mayonnaise
Romaine lettuce, washed and crisped

Slice the top off each apple and with a sharp spoon or knife hollow out the inside, leaving a ¼-inch shell. Soak in cold water until ready for use.

Remove all core from apple pulp and chop. Marinate apple pulp and nuts in mixture of oil, lemon juice and sugar for ½ hour. Drain and add the celery and mayonnaise. Pile into the apple shells and serve each on a romaine leaf. *6 servings.*

Citrus Salad

Very good with lamb or pork dishes.

1 head iceberg
   lettuce
½ head romaine
   lettuce
½ head chicory
1 cucumber
1½ cups grapefruit
   sections, canned
   or fresh
2 unpeeled red
   apples, cored and
   diced
½ teaspoon salt
1 tablespoon fresh
   mint, chopped
½ cup Lemon
   French Dress-
   ing, page 46

Wash and crisp the lettuces and tear into pieces. Peel, score and slice the cucumber. Drain grapefruit sections well. Toss lettuce, cucumber and grapefruit together with apples, salt and mint in a large wooden salad bowl. At the last minute pour on dressing and toss again. *8 servings.*

Celery and Chestnut Salad

This salad is especially good with game or poultry.

1 pound chestnuts
   Celery
1 jar (4 ounces)
   pimientos
½ cup Basic French
   Dressing, page 44

Slash the flat side of each chestnut and drop into boiling water. Boil 10 minutes, remove from heat and peel off shells and brown skin, holding under cold water to prevent burning your hands. Return to saucepan,

Lettuce leaves, washed and crisped

cover with fresh, salted boiling water and cook until barely tender, approximately 5 minutes. Cool and drain, then quarter. Place in a bowl and add an equal amount of finely chopped celery. Dice drained pimientos and add. Toss together with the French dressing. Heap onto lettuce leaves. *6 servings.*

Fruit Salad Bowl

This is a refreshing salad to serve with a heavy main course.

1 head romaine lettuce, washed and crisped
2 cups cantaloupe balls
2 cups honeydew balls
1 cup orange sections or slices
½ cup pineapple chunks, well drained
1 teaspoon salt
½ cup Sherry Dressing, page 59

Tear lettuce into bite-size pieces. Place in a wooden salad bowl with the fruit. Sprinkle with salt and pour dressing over all. Toss together lightly and serve immediately. *8 servings.*

Grapefruit and Green-Pepper Salad

Good with beef or lamb.

2 green peppers
3 tomatoes
1 large grapefruit
½ cup Basic French
Dressing, page 44
1 head lettuce of
your choice,
washed, crisped
and shredded

Seed green peppers and boil 5 minutes. Cool and cut lengthwise into julienne strips. Peel and seed tomatoes and cut pulp into strips. Peel grapefruit, removing all membrane; slice and remove seeds. Toss with dressing and serve on a bed of shredded lettuce. *6 servings.*

Grapefruit and Orange Mold

An excellent accompaniment for a rich casserole.

1 can (1 pound)
grapefruit sections
1 can (12 ounces)
mandarin oranges
Canned unsweet-
ened grapefruit
juice
2 envelopes (2
tablespoons) un-
flavored gelatin
½ cup cold water
1 cup sugar
½ cup boiling water
3 tablespoons
lemon juice

Drain grapefruit sections and mandarin oranges, reserving juices. Add to juices enough canned grapefruit juice to make 3 cups. Sprinkle gelatin on top of ½ cup cold water; let soften. Add sugar to ½ cup boiling water and bring to a boil, stirring until sugar has dissolved. Add softened gelatin and stir well until dissolved. Add the 3 cups of fruit juices and the lemon juice. Peel oranges, removing all membrane, and slice crosswise ¼ inch thick. Arrange orange slices on the bottom of a 1½-quart mold which has been rinsed in cold water.

2 seedless oranges
1 head Boston
  lettuce, washed
  and crisped

Pour in the gelatin mixture and allow to set until of egg-white consistency. Drop the grapefruit and mandarin orange sections into the gelatin and chill until firm. Unmold on a bed of lettuce. *6 to 8 servings.*

Mixed Fruit Salad or Cocktail

The secret of making this fruit salad is to use boiling-hot water to dissolve the sugar and steep the fruit. It is one of the best appetizers I can think of.

1 cantaloupe
2 apples
2 peaches
2 pears
3 plums
4 oranges
2 grapefruit
1 small bunch green
  grapes
½ pound cherries,
  pitted
1 cup sugar
  Boiling water

Seed cantaloupe and, using a small scoop, make as many balls as possible. Peel and dice apples, peaches, pears and plums. Peel and remove all membrane from oranges and grapefruit. Separate and halve the sections. Cut the grapes and cherries in half, removing seeds and pits. Pile fruits in a large glass or Pyrex bowl, sprinkle with sugar and pour on enough boiling water just to cover the fruit. Carefully turn fruit once or twice to distribute sugar, using a large wooden spoon. Place in the refrigerator for at least 12 hours before serving. *8 servings.*

Honeydew Rings

This is rather an impressive salad, so serve it when you can properly receive the compliments of your guests. It is a great asset to the buffet table.

1 package raspberry-flavored gelatin
2 cups boiling water
1 large ripe honeydew melon
1 apple, cubed
1 pear, cubed
1 peach, cubed
12 seedless grapes
1 package (12 ounces) cream cheese
Light cream
Chopped pecans
1 head romaine lettuce, washed and crisped

Dissolve gelatin in boiling water. Cool. Slice an end off the honeydew and with a long-handled spoon scoop out the seeds. Peel honeydew. Fill about three-quarters full of gelatin and refrigerate until filling has thickened to the consistency of egg white. Drop fruits into cavity. If cavity is not completely filled, add more gelatin. Chill until firm. (To prevent tipping, place melon in a heavy bowl in an upright position.)

Mash the cream cheese and dilute with a few drops of cream. Dry the melon well with paper toweling, then spread with the cream cheese, covering the entire surface. Roll in the chopped nuts. Chill again until cheese is very firm. With a sharp knife slice crosswise 1 inch thick. Line a platter with romaine lettuce and arrange the melon slices on it. *8 servings.*

Orange and Walnut Salad

Serve with duck or game.

4 cups seedless
oranges, peeled
and sliced cross-
wise ¼ inch thick
2 cups broken wal-
nut meats
3 tablespoons oil
¼ teaspoon salt
1 tablespoon lemon
juice
Watercress, if in
season, *or* lettuce
of your choice,
washed and
crisped

Place oranges and walnuts in a bowl and toss carefully with the oil, salt and lemon juice. Serve on a bed of watercress or lettuce. *8 servings.*

Tarragon Orange Slices

This salad complements roast duck admirably. It must be made with fresh tarragon.

6 large oranges,
peeled
1 head Boston let-
tuce, crisped and
shredded
Lemon French
Dressing, page 46
6 teaspoons chopped
fresh tarragon

Remove all white membrane from oranges and slice crosswise ¼ inch thick. Remove seeds, if any. Arrange on beds of shredded lettuce in 6 individual salad bowls. Pour a very small amount of dressing over oranges and sprinkle each serving with 1 teaspoon minced tarragon. Chill well. Serve with additional dressing. *6 servings.*

FRUIT SALADS TO BE SERVED AS DESSERT

Fresh Fruit in Champagne

1 cup sugar
¼ cup water
1 pint hulled and washed strawberries
3 peeled and diced peaches
2 peeled and sliced bananas
1 cup seedless green grapes
2 cups champagne
1 quart orange sherbet

Put sugar and water in a saucepan and bring to a boil, stirring constantly until sugar has dissolved. Place fruits in a handsome serving dish and pour the hot syrup over them. Cool. Pour champagne over the fruit, cover bowl and chill for several hours, or overnight. Just before serving drop scoops of sherbet into fruit and champagne and serve each person a little of each. *8 servings.*

Fruit Salad Trifle

1 No. 2 can pine-
apple tidbits,
drained
2 medium oranges,
pared and diced
2 peaches, pared,
pitted and diced
2 cups cubed stale
white cake, or
packaged lady
fingers
2 tablespoons dark
rum
Custard (below)
1 cup heavy cream,
whipped and
sweetened

Place fruits in a bowl and toss together. Break cake into bite-size pieces and place a layer in the bottom of a serving bowl. Sprinkle with rum, place one third of the fruit on top and spoon a thin layer of custard over this. Repeat process twice more, ending with a complete covering of custard. Chill thoroughly. Serve with whipped cream. *8 servings.*

Custard:

¼ cup sugar
¼ teaspoon salt
Dash of nutmeg
2 eggs, beaten
1½ cups milk
1 teaspoon vanilla

Combine all ingredients except vanilla in the top of a double boiler. Mix well. Cook over hot (not boiling) water, stirring constantly, for approximately 15 minutes, or until custard coats the back of a metal spoon. Remove from heat and cool. Add vanilla and stir well. *Makes 2 cups.*

Fruit Salad à la Creole

3 bananas
½ pineapple
4 oranges
½ cup superfine sugar
¼ cup rum
1½ quarts vanilla *or* peach ice cream
Chopped pistachio nuts

Peel bananas and dice. Peel and core pineapple and dice fruit. Peel oranges, removing all white membrane, and cut into thin circles. Place fruits in a bowl and toss with sugar. Sprinkle rum over all. Cover and place in refrigerator for several hours, turning occasionally with a wooden spoon. Place ice cream in a large deep serving dish and pour fruit over it. (Ice cream may be formed into balls with a serving scoop ahead of time and kept frozen, if so desired.) Sprinkle with pistachio nuts and serve. 8 *servings.*

Ginger Apples

¾ cup Scotch whiskey
½ teaspoon powdered ginger
8 cups apples, peeled, cored and sliced thin
1¼ cups sugar
Juice of 1 lemon
Juice of 1 lime
1 cup heavy cream, whipped and sweetened

Put whiskey and ginger in a jar and let steep 24 hours. Place apples in a heavy-bottomed pot. Pour ginger whiskey over them and add sugar, lemon juice and lime juice. Cook over medium-low heat until apples are transparent but not broken. Chill until very cold. Serve with whipped cream. 6 *servings.*

Mandarin Orange Dessert Salad

2 cans (11 ounces each) mandarin oranges
1 cup dairy sour cream
½ cup brown sugar, firmly packed
2 tablespoons dry sherry
Grated almonds

Drain mandarin oranges thoroughly and mix with sour cream. Fold in brown sugar and sherry. Chill very well. Sprinkle with almonds and serve. *4 servings.*

Orange-Banana Delight

½ cup orange juice
½ cup sherry
1 tablespoon lemon juice
½ cup sugar
1 egg white
3 bananas, peeled and diced
3 oranges, peeled and sliced
½ cup grated coconut

Put orange juice, sherry, lemon juice, sugar and egg white in a saucepan and bring to a boil, stirring constantly. Simmer, covered, 10 minutes. Strain and pour over mixed fruit. Chill well and serve sprinkled with the coconut. *6 servings.*

Pineapple Boat

1 large ripe pineapple
Superfine sugar
4 bananas
4 oranges
1 cup strawberries
Dressing (*below*)

Cut a lengthwise slice from one side of the pineapple, keeping the crown of leaves intact. Hollow out, cutting the fruit and core from the outer skin and leaving a shell about ½ inch thick. Sprinkle shell with superfine sugar and set aside.

Remove all core from the pineapple pulp and shred the fruit. Put in a glass, plastic or ceramic bowl. Slice bananas. Peel oranges and slice crosswise ¼ inch thick. Wash and hull strawberries. Add to the pineapple and pour the dressing over all. Chill in the refrigerator for at least 2 hours. Heap into the pineapple shell and serve. 6 *servings*.

Dressing:

1 cup sugar
½ cup water
3 egg yolks, well beaten
½ cup sherry
1 tablespoon lemon juice

Put sugar and water in the top of a double boiler over direct heat and heat, stirring, until sugar is dissolved. Boil uncovered for 5 minutes. Add a small amount of the syrup to the beaten egg yolks, beating constantly, then beat egg yolks into remaining syrup. Cook, stirring, over hot water in base of boiler until the mixture thickens slightly. Cool and add sherry and lemon juice. *Makes 1¾ cups.*

Turn-of-the-Century Rose Petal Salad

To be made when roses are in bloom. The petals add an exotic fragrance and flavor to this dessert salad.

2 cups freshly picked rose petals
1 cup port wine
1 cup heavy cream
2 peaches, pared and quartered
1 pint strawberries, hulled and washed
½ pound black cherries, halved and pitted
1 cup fine sugar
¼ cup confectioners' sugar

Stir 1 cup of rose petals into the port wine and 1 cup into the cream. Allow to mellow in the refrigerator for 2 hours. Place fruits in a bowl with the sugar and turn carefully to distribute the sugar evenly. Allow this, too, to steep in the refrigerator for 2 hours.

Strain wine and cream separately. Pour wine over the fruit. Place in a serving bowl. Whip cream until stiff, adding confectioners' sugar near end of beating. Serve as a sauce for the fruit. *8 servings.*

GLOSSARY

à la grecque: A style of cooking vegetables in a well-seasoned combination of oil, water and vinegar or other acid. The name probably refers to the Grecian origin of this method.

al dente: Italian term referring to the texture of vegetables or other foods (such as pasta) cooked to just the point where some resistance to the bite remains but the food can be considered cooked.

to bind: To hold a sauce together by adding egg, cream, cornstarch or other thickening.

to blanch: To pre-cook vegetables, fish, meats, etc. in boiling salted water for varying lengths of time.

bouquet garni: A seasoning bundle for foods to be cooked in liquid or by moist heat. Parsley, bay leaf and thyme are the basic components; recipes may specify other herbs, celery, etc., in addition. May be tied securely into a square of cheesecloth for easy removal of the herbs after use.

to clarify: To clear a liquid of sediment or cloudiness. Insures sparkling clearness for consommés and for meat, poultry or fish jelly for aspics.

court bouillon: Poaching liquid seasoned with onion, bay leaf, celery, parsley and sometimes other herbs. Used in preparation of fish, meats and poultry.

croutons: Small cubes of bread, either toasted or fried in butter or oil. Used to garnish soups and salads.

to emulsify: To cause oil particles to be suspended in a more or less stable mixture with a liquid or semisolid substance. Oil emulsifies when beaten steadily with egg in the making of mayonnaise.

to flute: To scallop the edges of vegetables or pastry.

to fold: To mix ingredients (often whipped eggs or cream) into a batter with a careful up and over motion, not a beating or stirring motion. This insures the maximum amount of air being retained in the batter.

forcemeat: A preparation of ground meats, herbs, other seasonings and sometimes vegetables or starches, used to stuff fowl, fish or meat.

galantine: A boned, stuffed and re-shaped bird that is poached, pressed and chilled before serving.

julienne: French term describing food cut into little thin strips.

macédoine: A preparation of several kinds of raw or cooked fruits or vegetables. May be served either hot or cold.

marinade: Any of various mixtures of oil with wine, vinegar or other acid, plus herbs and seasonings, used to tenderize meat or to flavor cooked vegetables for salads or other dishes.

to marinate: To steep in a marinade (*above*).

to mask: To coat a chilled cooked food with a thin layer of mayonnaise or other sauce.

mother: Term applied to the slippery mass of bacterial growth which causes cider or wine to ferment into vinegar.

to poach: To simmer gently in seasoned liquid until just cooked; method used for foods of delicate texture.

to purée: To reduce a food to a smooth pulp without adding liquid. Food may be puréed by being forced through a fine sieve or by being whirled in a blender.

to render: To extract fat from fatty animal tissues (as in making lard); the process is carried out over low heat.

to reduce: To boil down a sauce or a broth in order to strengthen the flavor or improve the consistency.

to sauté: To cook in a small amount of hot oil or butter over direct heat, with or without browning, as recipe directs.

to score: To slash very lightly through the outer surface of meat, vegetables or fruit, either with a knife or the tines of a fork.

to simmer: To cook in liquid over direct heat at a temperature below boiling; at simmering temperature, the surface of liquid shakes gently without bubbling.

to steep: To soak a food or flavoring in a liquid.

truffle: A subterranean fungus growth found only in France and northern Italy. Of exquisite flavor, especially when fresh, it is considered the epitome of garnishes and is extremely expensive.

to truss: To tie a fowl securely with string to prevent the legs and wings from protruding during cooking. Trussing helps prevent drying out of the bird.

vinaigrette: The French name of the oil and vinegar sauce popularly called "French dressing" in this country. There are many variations. In the name of a dish, "vinaigrette" indicates this style of preparation.

Index

ABOUT THE AUTHOR

BERYL M. MARTON is one of the most natural and most commonsensical of cooks. Her cooking school, the Yorktown Gourmet Cooking School, operated in her home, is especially popular with the busy housewife, inasmuch as she has a special ability to relate, à la Julia Child, to the problems of the aspiring hostess. Although more than proficient in all aspects of cuisine, including cooking chemistry, menu planning and gourmet cooking, her specialty is salads. And it just so happens that her husband manufactures high-quality kitchen ware, specializing in salad bowls. Mrs. Marton is known by many for her salad demonstrations in the leading department stores of the East, where women look forward to her informative, and often humorous, presentations.

In addition to her culinary skill, Mrs. Marton is an avid gardener—she grows many of her own herbs and vegetables—and ceramist. A Canadian by birth, she lives in Yorktown Heights with her husband and two teen-age sons, Bruce and Stewart.

HB9G